Scenarios for Success

directing your own career

To my husband Orv, who co-stars in our scenarios of love,
laughter, joy, and mutual support.

Rochelle

∾

To Mary Butler, who always believes in me.

Catherine

Scenarios for Success

directing your own career

Rochelle L. Teising
with Catherine Joseph

Rudi Publishing
San Francisco

Rudi Publishing, 12 Geary St., Suite 508, San Francisco CA 94108

ISBN 0-945213-30-1
First Edition

PRINTED IN THE UNITED STATES OF AMERICA
Vaughan Printing, Nashville TN

Library of Congress Cataloging-in-Publication Data

Teising, Rochelle L.,
    Scenarios for success : directing your own career / Rochelle L. Teising with Catherine
Joseph. -- 1st ed.
      p. cm.
    Includes bibliographical references and index.
    ISBN 0-945213-30-1
    1. Career development. 2. Success I. Joseph, Catherine.
II. Title.
HF5381.T255 1998
650.14--dc21   98-39652
                                    CIP

98   99   00   01   02   03   04   05   06   07   10 9 8 7 6 5 4 3 2 1

Kristin K. Boekhoff, Cover Designer
David Featherstone, Editor
Editorial Consultant: Joshua Bagby

Contents

Part Three   ACTION!

Chapter 7   The Editing Room

Chapter 8   Actor's Workshop

List of Exercises

Preface

I have spent more than twenty years helping thousands of people overcome obstacles to success in the workplace. My clients work in corporations, non-profit organizations, medical centers, legal and medical practice offices, technology and research firms, sales and marketing organizations, and public transportation and utility companies.

I work with people individually, in both private counseling and coaching sessions, and in groups through the seminars that I offer on-site in the workplace. As gratifying as it is to help people in these settings, I have wondered for some time how to reach—and help—a wider audience. The answer, it seemed to me, was to write a book in which I could share the techniques for breaking through the internal barriers to success.

Admittedly, a book on this topic is not an original idea. However, I think this book differs from other self-help books in several ways. First, this book, unlike others, focuses exclusively on being successful at work. The workplace presents unique challenges and demands, and the strategies for achieving success that you use in your personal life may prove ineffective, or even counterproductive, at work. Because you spend a significant amount of time at work, attaining success in the workplace can positively affect all others areas of your life.

Second, the book includes the metaphors I use in coaching people. These metaphors—to see your life as a movie, and your thoughts, words, and actions as the script for your life movie—are a creative approach to examining your barriers and making changes. Finally, the book includes a chapter on why it is so hard to let go of old ways of thinking and behaving, even when you really want to change. Most books do not address this issue, but I believe understanding why it is difficult to let go is the only way you can fully embrace new ways of behaving and can make lasting changes.

I am indebted to the work of Albert Ellis, the creator of rational emotive behavior therapy, and Martin E. P. Seligman, a pioneer in the study of optimistic and pessimistic thinking. Their work has greatly influenced my approach both to coaching people and to writing this book about how we create the scripts by which we live.

Writing a book is a challenging project. I am fortunate that my publisher introduced me to Catherine Joseph, who has helped me put my advice and insights into written words. Additionally, her experience in corporate management training and outplacement counseling has given her a familiarity with the issues and struggles people face in the workplace.

Thus, this book is truly a collaborative effort. It brings together my experience and expertise in counseling and coaching people to be more successful in the workplace and my co-author's expertise in writing. It also draws upon the insights from the many transitions and changes both of us have experienced in our own personal and professional lives. Together, we hope this book provides practical advice and direction to help you write your own scenarios for success.

Acknowledgments

I wish to thank the many friends and colleagues who helped and inspired me along my path, and particularly my clients from the many companies with whom I have consulted. Their struggles, courage, and triumphs have been my teacher. I also want to thank Linda Cohn and Sam Foster, my founding partners in Success at Work, as well as Robin Fine, Doris Harrison, Barbara Stern, David Lelewer, R. J. Valentino, and Sara Barnes. I offer deep appreciation to Eleanor Benelisha and Barbara Rose, my role models for living life with grace and dignity; to my husband, Orv, for his steadfast emotional support and contributions to shaping this book; to my three children, Barbara, Julie, and Mark, who continue to delight me with their successes in life; and to Max, Claire, and Anya, who keep me totally in present time with playful laughter and inquiring minds. My love and appreciation to you all.

Catherine Joseph wishes to thank Orv Teising, for his generous assistance typing transcripts and revisions and for his valuable suggestions; Don A. Rutherford, for his patience and loving support; Robert M. Robb, for his jokes and friendship; and Mary Butler, for her wisdom, insights, and encouragement.

We both wish to thank Terri A. Boekhoff of Rudi Publishing, who created the vision for this book and brought us together as collaborators; Josh Bagby for his contributions and movie references; Eta Burken and Michael Huston for their comments on the manuscript; and our editor, David Featherstone, for his revisions and advice.

Introduction

What keeps you from being as successful in the workplace as you want to be? What keeps you from achieving your potential?

I'm being blunt here. I'm assuming if you picked up this book, you want to be more successful at work. I ask the same question of my clients whom I coach for success.

My clients come to me unhappy, frustrated, even miserable and in pain. They want to do well, but they're struggling. A common theme I constantly encounter is that people—whatever the industry or organization in which they work—have difficulty overcoming obstacles to achieve success at work. Each person has a different scenario, but the theme is the same—each needs help to be successful at work.

Some people struggle to cope with an ever-changing workplace, where old, familiar rules for success are being replaced by new, unfamiliar rules. Other people face a variety of obstacles, such as tyrannical bosses, inflexible company policies, or a lack of tools and resources to get the job done.

Yet I find that the most significant obstacles to success are the negative, self-defeating beliefs and feelings people hold that prevent them from behaving successfully in the workplace. If you're struggling at work, you probably have obstacles like these, too.

In general, the external obstacles—bosses, company rules—are beyond your control. You don't have the power to change them. If that's the bad news, the good news is that the internal things—your beliefs, thoughts, feelings, and behavior—are well within your control to change.

The Old Beliefs and Patterns No Longer Work

Most people aren't aware that the beliefs, thought patterns, feelings, and behaviors they use on the job as adults were learned during childhood. Not surprisingly, the old beliefs and thought patterns that guided your life years ago don't work very well when you're dealing with today's work environment.

The first organizational structure you encountered was your family. That structure had a hierarchical order. One person—a parent—headed the group. Another person—another parent, perhaps—was the second-in-command. Below them were one or more people—the children—who had less power, or sometimes no power. The person on top, usually Dad, established the rules and wielded authority over the others in the group to make them abide by those rules. Can you see the parallel to your work setting?

Many problems you have in the workplace result from your unconscious attempts to duplicate the family structure you learned from childhood. It's an understandable model—it has a familiar structure, and it may be the only organizational structure you know. In the workplace drama, you unconsciously cast managers or supervisors in the mental and emotional roles of parents, and you cast co-workers as siblings. Then you take the ways you behaved in your family structure and use them in your work structure. And guess what—it doesn't work very well. But, it's the only way you know.

The Movie Metaphor

A scriptwriter puts characters into interesting situations, often embroiling them in conflict and stress. Much of the stress comes from the beliefs and attitudes the screenwriter instills in the characters. For example, a woman raised to be polite and efficient may be thrust into a job situation with a surly, obnoxious boss who never shows any outward signs of appreciation. You can imagine the problems that lie ahead in that pairing!

In the movies, the scripts are actual screenplays that actors follow. In real life, we follow scripts, too. We've unconsciously written our own scripts since childhood and continue to follow them to this day. Unlike actors, who get a new script for every new role, we use the same script over and over, even when we change job situations. We still take our beliefs and attitudes with us when we change locations and casts in the workplace.

When I listened to my clients describe their painful job situations, I would often think, Whoa, this sounds like a really bad movie! As my clients talked to me, I would envision their stories as if I were watching a movie. Then it dawned on me that we can approach dealing with life at work as if we were making a movie. It's a powerful metaphor that helps people understand what's going on in their lives.

I love the movies! I'm fascinated by the whole process that goes into moviemaking. I love how writers dream up situations and characters, and I love how actors breathe life into the words printed on the pages of a screenplay. I love how directors bring all the creative elements together to tell the story, and I admire the genius of producers who mastermind their productions. In our own life movie, we play all those roles. We dream up the stories of our life; we direct whatever action we take; we bring our scripts to life in our interactions with others; we mastermind the business of living.

In real life, we often think that events simply happen to us, and we don't realize how much control we can exercise in responding to them. Using the moviemaking metaphor, we can rewrite the script like a Hollywood scriptwriter. We can take the part of a director to analyze scenes and redirect ourselves in our new scripts.

When I share my moviemaking metaphor with my clients, it helps them put their career situations in perspective. As you'll discover in this book, thinking of your life in moviemaking terms can inspire you to take creative control. I'll show you how to rewrite your life script into an award-winning movie. I'll show you how to direct, star, and succeed in your own blockbuster— *My Successful Career!*

Lights! Camera! Action!

The process you go through when you make a change has three steps:

1. You shed light on what you're doing that prevents you from being successful.
2. You look at what you can do differently. You identify your options.
3. You choose a new way to do things.

The well known directive of "Lights, camera, action!" on a movie set parallels the three steps of making a change.

1. When you become aware of what you're doing, the *lights* go on.
2. When you look at what you can do differently and identify your

options, it's like using a *camera* to reframe the situation and focus on your options.

3. When you choose a new way to do things, you take *action*.

This book has thus been organized into three sections: Lights!, Camera!, Action! We'll look at what you can do at each step in the process to change your script.

Most self-help books concentrate on changing your behavior. Your behavior is the part of your script that is visible to the world, and it's the part to which other people—other *characters*—respond. For most people, however, the bulk of the work for change needs to be done with the invisible director inside the mind, with the area that controls and motivates behavior. Most of this book is about the invisible part. Once you are conscious of it, you'll know what you need to do to change your behavior.

This book presents many exercises designed to help you apply the information to your own situations. I suggest you keep a notebook or a pad of paper handy and use it to record your responses as you work through the exercises. As you begin, you may find it helpful to close your eyes, sit quietly for a few minutes, and think about your childhood, your parents, and any other adults such as aunts, uncles, grandparents, or sitters who cared for you or who played a big part in your life. Also think about the teachers, neighbors, or other adults you knew as a child. When you're ready, read through the questions and write down your responses. Take some time with these responses. You can begin with what you recall now and go back and fill in more information as it comes to you. This is a constantly evolving process. I'll refer to the exercises in later chapters, so number them for easy retrieval. It will become a record of your progress as you rewrite your scripts.

The characters you will read about in *Scenarios for Success* are based on the people I've worked with in my years of counseling. I've changed their names and altered their experiences enough to preserve their privacy, but the fundamental plot lines and the basic features of their scripts remain the same. Although each person's story is unique, they all share one thing: the old scripts they use sabotage their ability to be successful. Their stories will help you see that you're not alone in your struggles, and that others have felt similar pain and have overcome their invisible obstacles.

So, quiet on the set . . . ok. Everyone ready? Let's get started. "Lights!"

Part One

Lights!

Illuminate and Recognize
Your Old Scripts;
Discover the New Roles for
Success in the Workplace

Chapter 1

The Script Conference
Throwing the Spotlight on Your
Scripts From the Past

We begin our journey toward career success with a script conference. To follow our moviemaking metaphor, a script conference is where the director and scriptwriters meet to study the script. They often create a "back story," a glimpse at a given character's history showing why he or she thinks and behaves in certain ways—where did that snappy temper come from, or what fears control this character's actions? A back story helps the creative team establish a character's motivations, strengths, and weaknesses.

In creating your own metaphorical movie, *My Successful Career*, you'll do much the same thing. Of course, you won't have to invent a back story; instead, you'll cast light on the history you've already lived.

We begin our script conference in the workplace.

Andy, Nora, and Tony: Three People in Crises

Andy manages twenty-five people in a research firm. He's proud of the quality of work his department provides, and his staff enjoys a great reputation with senior management and other departments. Not far beneath the surface glitter, however, Andy's employees are frustrated and angry at him. A crucial decision must be made about one project's direction, and Andy won't commit to an answer. Jeff, one of the people who reports to Andy, asked in a recent staff meeting when they could expect a decision. Andy snarled at Jeff that it was impossible to make an informed decision when the staff had provided him with insufficient and inaccurate information. The staff groaned inwardly; they'd heard Andy's tirades before. They suspected that he couldn't make decisions and were losing faith in his ability to lead.

Nora has worked in the information security field for more than fifteen years. A bright, knowledgeable systems analyst, she works for a consulting firm that advises companies how best to protect their company and customer data. Although Nora is considered one of the best consultants in her field, her supervisor recently issued a disciplinary warning about her losing her temper with a client. This wasn't the first time she'd upset one of her clients. Nora has a growing reputation for creating chaos wherever she goes. She snaps at people, accuses them of incompetence, and pits one employee against another.

Tony is a sales representative for a health and disability insurance program designed for corporations. He has a knack for connecting with clients easily, identifying their needs quickly, and proposing logical, cost-effective solutions that please them. Unfortunately, he's not effective in following up on details to make sure the contract is complete. Twice last year, Tony's failure to follow up nearly cost the company big sales. His manager stepped in to save the sales and warned him that a third strike could cost Tony his job. Now another sale is teetering on the brink of slipping away due to Tony's weak follow-through, and his future with the company looks grim.

Andy, Nora, and Tony each face a crisis at work. Each thinks the problem is beyond his or her personal control: Andy feels frustrated by what he sees as his staff's lack of cooperation; Nora resents being warned about being unpleasant when she's just trying to do her job; Tony knows he's in trouble but doesn't know how to save himself.

Who's the Real Enemy, Anyway?

Some of my clients recognize that they create their own problems. They say things like, "I procrastinate," or "I'm uncomfortable asking for what I want," or "I don't feel I'm as good as my co-workers." These people may be aware of what's blocking them, but they may not be aware of why the blocks exist and what caused them. They know that what they're doing isn't working for them, but they can't think of what else they should do.

Andy, Nora, Tony, and countless others I've seen block their success with self-limiting beliefs about themselves and about the workplace. In most cases, they aren't even aware that they're beating themselves up with self-defeating thoughts and behaviors. For me, it's like watching a movie because I can see them following a script. You follow a script, too. If you're not happy with your career life, one of the first places to look for problems is in your script. This book will help you identify the self-limiting beliefs in your script and replace them with positive, self-affirming beliefs. That's how you are going to write your script for *My Successful Career.*

Understanding Your Belief System

Your belief system is the group of beliefs, assumptions, values, and attitudes you hold about how you believe the world works. It directs and influences who you are, and what you think, feel, and do. It's your view of yourself and the world—how you perceive the world and what you want it to be. Your belief system is the picture of reality you carry around inside your heart and mind. It's the invisible, ever-present director of the movie of your life, and it determines how successful you are.

We begin to develop our worldview as infants when we try making sense of this great new world. As growing children, we attempt to analyze and interpret the array of information, sensations, and events we experience. We hold as true what comes from the verbal and nonverbal messages and teachings we received from our parents, teachers, siblings, neighbors, and others we interacted with or observed. Our culture, religion, ethnicity, and socioeconomic class influence all our beliefs. Government and the media—including radio, television, newspapers, movies, and books—also influence us. By our adult years, we have a worldview that is embedded from our childhood experiences and how we interpreted them.

The world is a confusing place for a young child. At that age, you accepted on faith what you heard and were told; after all, these messages came from people you trusted and believed knew the truth. You didn't have the sophistication, analytical capability, or range of experience to decide if what your parents and other adults said was true or false.

When you heard your parents talking about politics, or current events, or what went on at work, you absorbed some of their views, values, and interpretations of their world. Perhaps you heard your father complain about work, snapping, "All bosses are jerks," or "You can't count on those people for anything." Maybe you overheard your mother complaining to a neighbor, "Women can't get a fair shake," or "No matter how hard we work, women can't get ahead in business."

Nonverbal messages were just as strong. Maybe your father toiled long hours and worked Saturdays and often missed your school plays or ball games. The nonverbal message you got as a child was that work is more important than family. Perhaps your mother stayed home to manage the house and rear you and your siblings. The nonverbal message there was that women belong at home.

As a child, you had not only limited exposure to the world, but also immature reasoning abilities. You misinterpreted things you saw and heard; you made incorrect assumptions. For example, a boy with a loving, supportive mother and a distant, aloof father may grow up assuming that all women have the same qualities he associates with his mother and all men have the same qualities he associates with his father.

Your vision of the world is unique to you. Each of us is an individual with different experiences and emotions. Although you may have grown up in a household with siblings who may share certain values and beliefs with you, you still have your own individual ways of interpreting your world. Gender, birth order among siblings, and personality account for the differences in our perceptions of reality.

Your belief system creates a template, or filter, through which you view, analyze, and interpret the experiences and events of your life. When something happens, you respond to it through the filter of your belief system. Metaphorically, this is a back story that motivates your behavior.

Who Runs Your Life?

While we've shed the clothes we wore as children, recognizing that they no longer fit, most of us have not recognized that our childhood beliefs don't fit us either. We're still using those viewing filters day in and day out, letting them influence key parts of our lives, including our career choices, work attitudes, and behaviors.

Would you trust a five or ten-year-old child to give insightful and accurate interpretations of the group dynamics operating in a staff meeting? This idea was the basis of the movie *Big*, starring Tom Hanks. In *Big*, a boy wakes up in a fully-grown adult body, and we see in comic fashion how he relates to an adult working world. As an adult, while you know the limitations of a child's interpretation of life, you may not realize that you still have your own set of childhood perceptual filters, and that they may be just as limiting.

Your worldview becomes a habit that you accept and, like most habits, seldom question. It helps you make sense of life, and most of the time it works fairly well. But when it doesn't, you've got problems! You cling to your familiar thinking patterns, not realizing how outmoded, inaccurate, or inappropriate they may be for you today. Beliefs are not inherently bad or good. Some, however, are productive and help you achieve what you want, while others are unproductive and prevent you from getting what you want.

Prudence was raised in a home where children were supposed to be seen and not heard. A timid and passive child, she grew up believing that success required pleasing others and not making waves. As a CPA, she suffered for years feeling invisible, used by her co-workers, and a failure in the corporate world. The internal director of the movie of her life would not let her see what a bright woman she was. After a coaching session with me, she understood immediately that those murky messages from her childhood were sabotaging her desire to shine at work.

History Repeats Itself

In movies, conflicts happen that make the characters confront their belief systems, often in an abrupt way. If voyagers on *Star Trek* didn't have the ability to adjust to different planetary perspectives with alacrity, they'd be in deeper trouble than usual. In our everyday lives on Earth, we rarely question our worldview. We rarely wonder where our beliefs come from and whether they still serve us as adults.

We're often creatures of habit. There's a story about a teenage girl who watched her mother prepare a pot roast and finally asked, "Mom, why do you always cut off the ends of the roast?"

"That's the way you make pot roast, dear. That's how my mother always did it."

A few days later, the girl asked her grandmother why she always cut off the ends of the pot roast. "Oh, I had a small roasting pan," her grandmother replied. "I always cut off the ends of the roast to make it fit."

More than we'd like to admit, we cut off parts of ourselves to fit into the roasting pan of our parents' or teachers' expectations. Perhaps as children we cut off our natural curiosity about trying new things because our parents detested change. We became so accustomed to suppressing curiosity or creativity that we've forgotten how much we changed to please them.

As adults, we assume we know what truth and reality are. But whenever I recall childhood events with my siblings, or listen to my children describe episodes from their youth, I marvel at how each speaker shares a different memory of the same event. In both real-life and in movie detective stories and courtroom dramas, a common theme is trying to decide what really happened, because two people telling what they believe is the truth may have conflicting accounts of reality.

A couple recalling the early days of their courtship may tell different stories. She says, "You waited a week after you met me before you called for a date, and then you showed up a half-hour late." He says, "You told me not to call you right away and warned me not to arrive before eight o'clock." Whose version is the truth?

These different memories and interpretations of the same event are what we call *reality*. Reality is actually very fluid. There is no one, single, true way things happened, nor one, single, true interpretation. We each observe and interpret events through our personal filter—the lens through which the invisible director in our mind views our life movie. Our reality is whatever we think it is. It can change as our memory changes, as new information flows in, or as our understanding of the world changes.

Remember that classic Frank Capra film *It's a Wonderful Life,* starring Jimmy Stewart? With his life in shambles on Christmas Eve, George Bailey thought he was a failure, so much so that he was bent on suicide. He was saved by Clarence, his guardian angel, who showed George through some heavenly magic that he had made a tremendous difference in the lives of people in his home town of Bedford Falls. George had such a perceptual awakening that he was able to look back at his history in a whole new way. His shift in thinking inspired him to live again and to realize what a success he was!

We each decide what the truth is. We decide *the way it is* or *the way it should be.* As the director of our life movie, we create a screenplay that is in harmony with our beliefs and attitudes. What you believe is what you get!

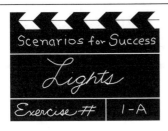

Scenarios for Success
Lights
Exercise # | 1-A

What Are Your Beliefs?

1. Listed below are beliefs I often hear people express. Check which ones you also believe.

☐ I'm a loyal employee, and I will stay here no matter what.

☐ I'll never get what I want because ___ (fill in the blank).

☐ I don't deserve to be successful.

☐ If I'm successful, I won't be who I really am.

☐ I'm doing better than my parents did at my age, so I shouldn't complain.

☐ It upsets me when others don't like me.

☐ Change is scary. Change brings problems.

☐ It's management's job to solve the problems.

☐ I don't think I should have to take directives from anyone.

☐ Politics is what determines your success at work.

☐ Companies should put their people first and take care of them.

☐ I can't help being miserable.

☐ It's not my fault things are bad.

☐ I have to keep working hard to get ahead.

☐ A lot of people rely on me, and I have to take care of them before I can care for myself.

☐ It's embarrassing to be wrong.

☐ Security is the most important thing in a job.

☐ Other people prevent me from being as successful as I could be.

☐ People are basically lazy and selfish creatures who can't be trusted.

☐ Asking for help at work makes one vulnerable.

☐ Work is a drag.

☐ Life should always be easy.

☐ Life is a burden; life is about struggle and pain.

☐ Life should be fair.

☐ There's only so much room at the top. Not everyone can be successful.

☐ The people at work are like my family.

☐ Unless you are a certain skin color, gender, age, or weight, you can't expect to get ahead.

☐ I have a difficult life, and it's unfair for others to expect a lot from me.

☐ I'm a perfectionist.

☐ It really doesn't matter what I do because I'll never get ahead.

☐ I'm afraid if people get too close to me, they'll find out that I'm a fake.

☐ If I start being really successful, my spouse or partner will be hurt or jealous.

☐ If I collaborate with others, I'll be giving my power away.

☐ When you work in teams, you don't get individual credit for your work.

☐ No matter how hard I work, I can't get ahead.

☐ Other people have power over my life.

2. Where did these beliefs come from? As you review each belief, what messages from your parents or other adults come to mind? What child-hood memories come up that relate to this belief?

Our Scripts from the Past

The scripts you developed during your childhood are still in use today. By *scripts*, I mean your thoughts, feelings, and behaviors. As children, we crafted strategies utilizing these elements to get what we wanted, to avoid getting hurt, and to deal with fears. These strategies became scripts that still determine how we will react and what we will do in various situations. Here are some examples:

> We think: If I can't get my way . . .
> . . . I'll leave.
> . . . I'll stay but I'll withdraw verbally.
> . . . I'll pout.
> . . . I'll complain loudly.
> . . . I'll attack verbally.
> Or think: If something or someone gives me too much trouble . . .
> . . . I'll be sick that day.
> . . . I'll procrastinate.
> . . . I'll avoid talking to them.
> . . . I'll complain about how unfair things are.

Ghostwriters

Just like many movie scripts, these life scripts are the result of a collaborative effort. Unfortunately, we don't know who all the collaborators were. The basic script reflects the culture we grew up in. The writing team included our parents and their parents, our siblings, relatives, teachers, close friends, and many others from our childhood. I call all these people "ghostwriters" because their influence and impact on our scripts are often invisible.

Even though we are adults, we still respond to the influences of our ghostwriters. Sometimes we recognize their influence. For example, a man religiously spends an hour every Sunday evening reviewing notes for the project he's working on and mentally preparing himself for work on Monday. He does this because he remembers his father doing it—"A smart businessman has to be sharp and ready to hit the ground running at eight o'clock. Monday morning!" He knows that his father's script has become his own.

Most of the time, however, we are unaware of the scripts we enact, and we don't stop to consider who wrote them. Our parents and ancestors may be long gone or far away, but their lessons and messages live on in our scripts. We continue to act out their scenarios in our adult life.

Clients have said to me things such as, "I won't work for a woman manager," "Never trust management," or "Let the boss make the decisions. That's what he gets paid for." When I ask where these ideas came from, they think for a minute and say, "That's something my father used to say," or "I remember hearing my grandmother say that." Ask your father why he always said a certain thing, and he might tell you that his father or another close relative said it. We may have lost track long ago of the origin of the messages that still hold the power to shape us and influence our actions today.

Let me summarize the points I have made so far. If you are like most people:

- Your beliefs run you and dictate your scripts.
- You rarely question whether you could write a new script or play another role because you rarely question your beliefs.
- Most of the time, you operate on automatic.

Beliefs and Scripts Can Change

Do our beliefs and scripts ever change? Yes! They change when we are exposed to different life experiences. Education, travel, interaction with people who have different beliefs and values, television, and the Internet are all things that may change your beliefs. Anything that broadens your horizons, pops you out of the box, and exposes you to different ways of thinking can make you revise your beliefs and your scripts.

Stories abound of how teachers have inspired changes in children's beliefs about themselves. A ten-year-old boy rarely spoke in school because the other children made fun of his stutter. Ashamed, he believed he would never be able to speak normally. One day his teacher asked him to stay after school. She handed him a book and asked him to read to her while she corrected papers. He stuttered through the first two paragraphs of the book and then stopped, embarrassed by his difficulty in reading aloud. The teacher continued to correct papers and said, "You have a beautiful voice. Please keep reading to me." The boy continued to read aloud, still stuttering. Finally the teacher said, "Thank you. I like the sound of your voice. Will you read to me tomorrow?"

The boy read to her after school every day for the rest of the school year. His teacher said nothing as he read, but simply listened to him as she corrected papers. At the end of the half hour, she would say, "You have a beautiful voice. I enjoy hearing you read."

You're probably not surprised to hear that the boy grew up to become a radio announcer. He credits his fifth grade teacher for helping him change his debilitating beliefs.

Outdated Scripts in the Workplace

We physically separate from our parents and families when we grow up and move away from home, but we still are connected emotionally through our scripts. We also still have issues from our family that have not been fully resolved and needs that were not completely met in childhood.

We bring our scripts, unresolved issues, and unmet needs with us into any new relationships we create, both personal and professional; when we do this, we unintentionally re-create many of the same problems we had in our family setting. Here's an illustration of what happens when we bring these unconscious scripts into the work setting.

Carly felt rejected as a child by her cool, aloof parents. To win their approval, she would try to be as cheerful and helpful as possible. She'd run to bring her mother a cup of tea without being asked, and she'd offer to wash the car for her father. Today, she still strives to win the approval of her managers and co-workers by being helpful. She brings home-baked cookies to staff meetings. She organizes birthday celebrations for co-workers, buying the card and getting everyone to sign it. She has a ready ear and shoulder to cry on for anyone having problems.

Last year, Carly was appointed to a committee to study the feasibility of a new project. When the project was approved, she expected her manager to appoint her to the project team. He didn't. Carly instantly felt devastated. She felt rejected by her boss and the project team members, just as she felt rejected by her family. Her belief was that if she took care of other people, they would take care of her. The script she learned from her family did not create success for her in the workplace.

Characters in the Workplace

Babies cry "Waaah!" when they want attention or are afraid and need reassurance. While we learn as we grow up that "Waaah!" usually won't get our needs met anymore, we still have similar core needs we had as babies. We keep looking to fulfill our needs for love, attention, approval and security. We see a

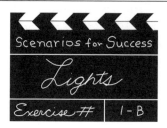

Beliefs About Work

1. When you consider them in the context of your work experience, what reactions do you have to the following terms? For example, the word *money* might trigger the following: "Money is the root of all evil." "You can never have enough money." "Money makes people greedy." "I want to earn more money." "It's wise to save money."

Write down your reactions to the following:
> Money
> Authority
> Success
> Failure
> Work
> Responsibility
> Promotions
> Power
> Competition
> Ambition

2. What messages about these topics did you get from your parents, relatives, teachers, and other adults as you were growing up? How do they compare to yours?

3. The reactions you wrote down are your beliefs about these topics. How do these beliefs help or hinder you at work?

whole range of behaviors in the workplace as people strive to fulfill their needs. Some managers have trouble delegating because they need to control everything; other managers have such a laissez-faire approach they seem completely uninvolved with their staff. We see perfectionists and procrastinators. Some people become paralyzed because they're afraid to make the wrong decision; others make impulsive decisions because they can't stand unresolved issues. Some people drive others crazy by asking too many questions about every little thing; others ask nothing and just detach themselves from the situation. Some people have difficulty receiving praise and recognition; others can't function well without it.

We find people who are overly involved with co-workers' personal problems and who act as surrogate therapists. Other workers totally disregard the feelings of co-workers and don't appear to care about anybody else. Some people are very emotional, while others are very controlled, displaying no emotions at all. We see caretaking types who go overboard to the point of assuming responsibility for the mistakes of others and covering for those who aren't doing well; we also see those who constantly look for someone to take care of them.

Entering an office in today's workplace is like going to Central Casting in Hollywood. All the people play out the scripts they learned from their family history and brought into the workplace. They have cast their co-workers and managers into the parts once played by their siblings and parents.

People behave as they do because their belief system tells them what they need or don't need from others. They see others through their own filters. As you read through the behaviors in the previous paragraph, you may have thought of people at work to fit each type. You used your unique belief system to identify someone as a perfectionist or as a procrastinator. The beliefs you have about your co-workers and your manager might change if you have different information about them.

Why You Are Who You Are Today

You are a product of the family environment in which you grew up. If you came from a home where an inordinate amount of responsibility was placed on you at an early age, you could become an adult with an overly developed sense of responsibility, or a workaholic driving yourself toward burnout because you don't believe you've made it. Or you could go in the other direction, shirking responsibility as an adult, and seeking the freedom you feel you were denied as a child. You also may have problems meeting deadlines, fulfilling work commitments, or showing up for work at all.

If you were rewarded as a child for being quiet at home, you may now be a compliant, invisible worker, unconsciously still seeking approval and rewards from your managers for not creating trouble. If you grew up in a family where love was withheld and you had to compete with your brothers and sisters for your parents' attention and approval, as an adult you may feel you now must compete with your co-workers for the boss's attention and approval. If you were habitually late to school and band lessons, perhaps in defiance of strict parents or because you wanted to command attention, you may still be arriving late to work and staff meetings. If you delight in reporting other employees who go against company policy, perhaps you ran to your parents as a child to tattle on your siblings or got rewarded from your teachers for reporting classmates who cheated on tests. The roles you learned to play as a child are the same roles you are playing at work today.

Treating Your Boss as You Treated Your Parents

Many people unconsciously project feelings about their parents onto people in positions of authority in their organizations. Kids who defied authority and rebelled against their parents often do the same thing in the workplace as adults, defying company policies and rebelling against their bosses. Children who felt powerless interacting with their parents have trouble as adults confronting their bosses at work. The anger, helplessness, or dependency needs children experienced with their parents often get played out with supervisors, while conflicts and power struggles with siblings re-create themselves in dramas with co-workers.

Meanwhile, bosses play out unresolved issues from their own family experiences as well, like Andy, who frustrates his staff with his inability to make timely decisions. He had parents who found fault with almost every thing. They had demanding standards by which they measured Andy, and they made it clear to him that anything less than excellence was unacceptable. When Andy made a mistake, his father would call him a stupid idiot and say sternly, "If you'd stopped to think, this wouldn't have happened." To encourage Andy not to settle for second best, they pointed out all the ways he could improve himself and do better next time. When they watched the news on television, his parents would make disparaging comments such as, "Most people are fools."

Naturally, Andy developed beliefs that anything less than perfection was not good enough, that failures or mistakes were signs of stupidity and weakness, and that most people were incompetent. These beliefs became the foundation for his script and the role he played at work. His script compelled him not to trust others for information because they might be ignorant or incompetent. He hesitated to make decisions for fear he might make a bad one and become the fool his parents disparaged.

How People Sabotage Themselves

I've seen many ways that people sabotage themselves in the workplace and unconsciously limit their chances for success. Here are some of them:
- Procrastination
- Uncontrolled anger; verbally abusing others
- Not participating; being moody and unresponsive
- Doing only what is asked
- Ego trips and empire-building
- Playing the victim
- Over reacting to situations; taking everything personally
- Resisting change; fearful of taking risks; being afraid to change jobs
- Personality conflicts with co-workers and bosses
- Getting sexually involved with co-workers
- Habitual tardiness
- Negative attitude; constant complaining; hostility; a chip on their shoulder

I'm sure many of these behaviors are familiar to you. They all have roots in the old scripts from childhood that we bring into the workplace.

When Scripts Collide, Fireworks Explode

In writing a movie, a screenwriter creates the essence of drama by placing a character with one script squarely in the path of another character with a radically different script. Drama ignites as the scripts collide.

This happens frequently in the workplace, too. We all bring our old scripts, roles, unresolved issues, and unmet needs into the work environment. When these collide, they can ignite drama, often with dire consequences. When an employee and manager reach an impasse, you'll usually find a script collision at the root of it.

Recently, I worked with Audrey, an insecure employee who constantly sought reassurance that her work was acceptable. Her manager, Phil, had a very hands-off style and saw her requests as childish and immature. The more Audrey pushed for approval, the further Phil retreated; the more he pulled back, the more needy for attention she became. By the time I intervened, Audrey was distraught, thinking Phil was ignoring her, and he was irritated that she was so demanding and intrusive.

I saw them individually to examine their different perspectives, old needs, and struggles—from their back stories. Audrey's insecurity resulted from her emotionally distant parents. She was desperate to get attention and approval from anyone in authority. She played out the same role with her manager that she played with her unavailable parents.

Phil grew up with a mother who incessantly demanded his attention and care. As a boy, he felt his mother constantly intruded on his time and thoughts. Consequently, he recoiled when any employee, particularly a woman, demanded his attention. Phil enacted the same role with his employees he had with his mother.

We are scripted to react to certain character traits and situations. For example, someone habitually manipulated by her parents will react negatively to a co-worker she thinks is trying to manipulate her. A manager who felt criticized by his parents or teachers will not take well to an employee who points out problems in the department and will view the employee's statements as a criticism of his management abilities. A child who was the object of his parents' excessive attention and was lavished with gifts and material things may, as an adult, act as if he is entitled to raises, perks, and promotions without performing his job responsibly.

The situation becomes more complex as more people and scripts become involved. Yvette, a manager who grew up in a household with frequently absent and neglectful parents, has trouble today discussing performance problems with her staff. Yvette internally struggles with approval and rejection and is afraid her staff won't like her. Meanwhile, one of her employees "gets away with murder." Van, who has unresolved issues with a very authoritarian father, feels no one has the right to tell him what to do. When Yvette gives him a directive, he ignores it. Yvette wants to be liked so much that she hesitates to confront him.

Allison often complains of headaches that make it difficult for her to concentrate on her work. She is often out sick and does not handle job stress well. Allison learned as a child that if she acted sick when she felt overwhelmed, her mother would not make her do household chores. Yvette's reluctance to speak to Allison affects yet another employee, Owen, who resents Yvette for not confronting Allison and Van. He resents covering for the poor efforts of his co-workers, yet since he grew up in a home where people never told the truth to each other, he won't speak directly to Yvette. Instead, he complains bitterly about his manager to any co-worker who will listen.

Some managers assume a parental role and respond to their staff the way their parents responded to their children. They may be protective of younger staff members, even making excuses for them. Or they may duplicate the authoritarian stance of their parents, demanding compliance, distrusting their staff, and being unwilling to entertain employees' suggestions or ideas.

Another major area where scripts collide is when romance intersects with office life. Bonita enjoyed her challenging work in a male-dominated stock brokerage firm, and she also liked the flirting and attention she attracted as a comely woman. She was especially attracted to Mitch. After several weeks of working together, Bonita joined Mitch after work for drinks in a nearby bar. One smile led to another, one kiss led to another, and later that night she accompanied him to his place.

Their scripts collided after the sexual intimacy of that night. When Bonita returned to work the next morning, she believed that she and Mitch were now a couple. Mitch had no such belief. He became aloof to her at the office and behaved as though no intimacy had occurred between them. He wasn't ready to pursue a relationship and found Bonita's provocative advances unprofessional and smothering. Bonita, coming from a painful background of sexual abuse, struggled with Mitch's rejection and felt used and victimized. By the time she came to see me for help, she was desperately making phone calls trying to reconnect with Mitch, who by then was ready to file harassment charges against her.

Dozens of Movies Play Simultaneously

Each of us stars in our own script. We get so absorbed in our own issues, our own struggles, and our own movies—both the movies in our mind and the movies we are living in—that it often doesn't dawn on us that other people's scripts and other people's movies are showing simultaneously. Ours is not the only show in town!

Our boss is not our father or mother; our co-workers are not our siblings. Our beliefs and emotions are connected to the old cast of family characters, not to the present cast of our managers and co-workers. Yet we still continue to play out the roles we learned as children in a dogged attempt to get from the people in the workplace what we didn't get from our parents. Our underlying belief is that if I keep doing this and this and this, then maybe I'll get what I need. Sometimes we even pump up the intensity of the script—we do the same thing, but louder, more emotionally, or more energetically—in a misplaced hope that this time it will work.

When I started kindergarten, my mother used to listen to soap operas on the radio. When I'd be home from school sick, I'd listen to them, too. Although I heard the soaps only a few times a year, I heard the same basic plot and the same characters bemoaning the same problems time after time. The scenarios didn't change much from year to year. Even when the soap operas moved to television the scenarios were the same. It's often like that with our own scenarios. We get older, we change jobs, we have a different boss; but our soap operas stay much the same. We keep trying to get what we want in ways that might have worked when we were children, but they don't work now that we are adults.

Most of us don't set out consciously to sabotage or punish ourselves, and yet we often get stuck in self-punishing, self-sabotaging behavior. Even when we recognize we are hurting ourselves, we often still persist in playing the scripts that cause us pain. Although our scripts are failing us, we continue, blindly, to follow them.

Lab rats in a maze quickly learn which paths lead to a chunk of cheese. They don't keep going down paths that have no reward at the end. Human beings, on the other hand, will pursue paths or repeat behaviors that constantly yield disappointment. It makes one wonder if lab rats are smarter than humans. We humans persist in repeating behaviors and following scripts to nowhere because we stubbornly cling to our belief that maybe, this time, we'll get lucky. Charles Schultz brilliantly illustrates this concept in his *Peanuts* comic strip. Lucy always pulls away the football just as Charlie Brown kicks at it. *Ka-Plomp!* Yet Charlie Brown persists in believing that next time Lucy will play by the rules.

Marlena's mother was a self-centered, embittered woman unable to give her children the love and attention they needed. As a child, Marlena yearned for her mother's affection and concern. The only reliable way for her to get her mother's attention was to get sick. Marlena clung to her belief system as she grew older, not realizing how outmoded it was becoming.

Recently, Marlena was working on a marketing plan with a colleague. Cynthia had done much of the preliminary work, which she described at length to Marlena. Suddenly, Marlena began to have trouble breathing. After a half-hour of gasping for air, she became alarmed and called her doctor. He told her to meet him at the emergency room. As Marlena prepared to leave, Cynthia expressed concern about Marlena's ability to drive to the hospital in a wheezing state. Marlena assured her she would be fine. When she saw her doctor, he diagnosed her problem as an asthma attack and gave her the proper medication.

A week later, Marlena met with Cynthia to continue work on the project. When Marlena arrived, Cynthia immediately began talking about the project and what still needed to be done. Marlena became increasingly upset that Cynthia talked about the project and did not ask her how she was feeling or what had happened to her at the hospital the week before.

Why was Marlena so upset? The asthmatic episode had triggered Marlena's longing for her mother's attention. As Cynthia talked business, Marlena thought, "She hasn't asked how I am and what happened at the hospital. She's going on as if nothing happened. She doesn't care about me. She doesn't like me. I don't matter. She's simply using me to advance her own career." All this flashed through her head in an instant. Marlena wasn't aware of the string of thoughts, just the theme, and she felt hurt and neglected. When Cynthia finished describing her idea and asked what she thought, Marlena's first impulse was, "What does she care about what I think? Since I don't matter to her, she must be asking my opinion just to be nice, not because she values my viewpoint."

Let's freeze this scene for a moment. Marlena used an old childhood script to interpret a present-day event. Was the script appropriate? No, it was not. Cynthia did care about Marlena; but her focus was on the task at hand and she really wanted to hear Marlena's opinion. Marlena had worked herself into a frenzy by resurrecting her feelings and past behavior patterns. Her old script had caused her to misread Cynthia completely. She created needless anguish for herself and risked damaging her working relationship with Cynthia.

Unrealistic Expectations

Frequently the pain we experience in our lives is the difference between our expectations and reality. In the workplace, the discomfort, unhappiness, and dissatisfaction we feel often takes place because our unique picture of how things should be isn't happening. Typically, we have expectations about high rewards, about what management should do for us, and about how our co-workers should treat us.

We base these expectations on our family code of what was rewarded at home and what we were told—and have come to *believe*—should happen at work. I often see clients who have logged many years of loyal work at a company. They are hurt because they've never been promoted. They expect that loyalty and reliability should be rewarded, and it clouds their ability to see that the people earning the promotions work harder, are smarter, bring in much-needed skills, or have political savvy. A promotion frequently has nothing to do with loyalty or longevity!

One client of mine was upset that his manager didn't include him in meetings. I asked, "What have you done to make yourself visible so that your presence is desired at these meetings? Have you asked your manager to invite you?" He replied, "My manager should know that I want to attend." He put the responsibility on the manager to mind-read his expectations.

Janet believed she was a great team player. As part of a team of nurses, she always offered to help others with their duties whenever she'd completed her own. When the other nurses finished their duties, they took a break or made a personal call. This infuriated Janet. Her family had a rule: when your own work is done, you help others. All her siblings shared in helping each other complete their household tasks. Janet brought this expectation into the workplace, but it wasn't shared by others. Unaware of the source of her rage, Janet made snippy, sarcastic comments to her fellow nurses and quickly became regarded as a problem employee. Had she recognized her own code and personal expectations for what they were, she could have changed her behavior and avoided being labeled as a troublemaker.

Not all the expectations we bring to the workplace are unrealistic. The expectations that one should be adequately compensated for one's work, that a manager should treat employees with fairness and respect, and that co-workers should set aside personal differences to focus on team goals are not unrealistic. However, as Janet discovered, it *is* unrealistic to assume that everyone in the workplace plays by the same rules and has the same expectations. We cause ourselves much grief when we mistakenly assume that because we all work in the same department or on the same team, we share the same expectations and belief systems. The hurt, anger, and frustrations come from thinking that it's someone else's fault that the reality of the workplace doesn't match our expectations.

Scenarios for Success

Lights

Exercise # 1-C

What Scripts Are You Using?

1. Think about how you responded to the following situations when you were a child. Make some notes about how you handled these situations.

- Being criticized by an adult, such as a parent or teacher
- Being criticized by another child, such as a sibling or classmate
- Giving criticism to others
- Competing with siblings for your parents' attention
- Being ignored, neglected, left out
- Encountering something new, such as the first day of school, or a stranger
- Doing something for the first time, such as bike riding or swimming
- Feeling anger
- Being afraid
- Having hurt feelings
- Being jealous
- Coping with stress
- Meeting deadlines for school projects
- Asking for help
- Being asked for help

2. What parallels do you see with how you now handle these situations as an adult in the workplace?

Unrealistically high standards and expectations of ourselves can also cause us pain, grief, and misery. When we can't meet our own self-created expectations, we feel like failures. Instead of recognizing that our expectations are so unrealistic no one could attain them, we berate ourselves and work ourselves into frustration.

The High Price We Pay for Our Old, Outdated Scripts

What does the movie of your career look like? If it looks like a horror film or a tragedy, you're a great candidate for looking at your behaviors and old roles to see what changes you can make. We pay a high price for our self-defeating behaviors and our outdated scripts. They sabotage our chances for success. The price we pay can be measured in negative terms: raises or promotions we didn't get, loss of status, poor self-image, frustration, unhappiness, or illness.

Part of the price is expressed in emotional ways: anxiety, loneliness, low self-esteem, inadequacy, approval-seeking, insecurity, anger, resentment, bitterness, humiliation, depression, procrastination, indecisiveness, impulsiveness, perfectionism, guilt, and hatred.

Another part of the price we pay for relying on outdated scripts is physical: hypertension, chronic pain, burnout, exhaustion, migraines, ulcers, stroke, drug and alcohol problems, and eating disorders. For people who come from unhappy families where one or both parents were emotionally unavailable due to alcoholism, illness, or divorce, the consequences may be more dramatic.

We pay in other ways, too, such as missing opportunities to develop satisfying personal relationships, to achieve inner peace, to continue to grow and learn, or to reach personal goals.

We are not the only ones who pay a high price. Our spouses and children also suffer. Meanwhile, the workplace is like a home away from home. Sometimes we see our co-workers more than we see our family. Suffering and misery spreads through the workplace like a disease and creates a toxic environment that affects everyone's productivity. Everyone involved gets cast to play roles in the melodrama, *My Horrible Career.*

It's Time for a Change

We need to transform the workplace into a place of creativity and joy, where people have the emotional maturity to get the job done. The way to start is by recognizing and overcoming the blocking, or self-defeating, beliefs and scripts that are preventing you from achieving your maximum potential.

Your scripts have enabled you to get where you are today, and we want to honor how they have helped you get this far. Yet if you struggle and suffer in the workplace, you should consider whether those old scripts still work in your favor. It's a different world now than it was when you first wrote those scripts many years ago. For one thing, the workplace has changed dramatically over the past few years. For another, *you* have changed, too. You are no longer a child, reliant upon adults for basic necessities, and the mental scripts you wrote when you were six years old no longer fit today.

It's time to write your new scenarios for success so you can direct and star in *My Successful Career*. The first step in writing your new script is to pull down the old ones from the script archives in your mind. Awareness is the first step to change. You need to become aware of what you've been doing. You want to look back at your history to see how your belief systems were created and how your scripts came to be written. You need to look at the back story of your movie. As you do this, you'll develop new ways of thinking and behaving that are more appropriate for you as an adult in the work environment. You'll learn how to be a good actor for your script, as well as a good director and producer. Let's head to Central Casting.

Chapter 2

Central Casting

Identifying the Traits for Professional Success in Workplace 2000

An actor's job is to take words of dialogue and action printed on a page and bring them to life in a compelling, and convincing way. To do this, an actor must study not only the character's lines, but also the setting for the movie. If you were going to play a prospector in the gold rush, you'd want to study what life was like in California in 1849. Gathering this background information would help you create a believable character.

In working on your new movie, *My Successful Career*, you want to study what the working environment is like for a successful worker in the twenty-first century. This chapter presents background information about the new world of work for whatever role you will play in it.

No matter what your job—from a waitress in a doughnut shop to astrophysicist, and no matter where you work—from corner video store to a multinational corporation—the world of work is changing.

Traditional job descriptions that told you exactly what to do are fading into antiquity. Today, you're more likely to get a list of your performance expectations for the year, yet even these performance expectations don't tell the whole story of what managers want or what is required for success in the workplace. Although you may possess the skills, knowledge, and aptitude to do the job, your success may hinge on showing you have the attributes managers want and that your workplace demands.

If you've been in the workforce for a while, you've seen the changes coming. If you're fairly new to the working world, you may still be adjusting to an environment that's decidedly different from life at home and school. Wherever you are in your career, success requires that you know the new rules of the workplace and what employers look for these days.

Changes In the Workplace

In the movie of your life, *My Successful Career*, the setting of the twenty-first century features a bold new working environment. Far-reaching changes with enormous implications for all of us have taken place, and many of us are still struggling to adjust to them. The changes include the following:

- A new global economy
- Increased competition
- Rapid advances in information technology
- Mergers, restructurings, and downsizings
- Increased automation
- Outsourcing of non–revenue-producing jobs

These changes are forcing companies to rewrite their scripts for conducting business and are bringing an end to the era of job security. Companies used to have a large cast of characters; now they have a small cast. Automation and outsourcing have reduced or eliminated the supporting cast, and now every member of the cast must add value to the organization and be a fully contributing player.

Many beliefs, assumptions, and expectations you developed about work were formed during a past economy and workplace. Those days have gone the way of electric typewriters and carbon paper. It's a new game now.

In the traditional employment contract of the past, employees traded their loyalty, dependability, observance of rules, and many years of service for job security. It was often like a long-term marriage. In the late 1970s, those contracts began to fade to black and today have all but vanished. The new script for business calls for employees to be in charge of their own career destinies. Now you are rewarded for keeping abreast of changes, being creative, and having the current skills that companies need.

Many big organizations have decentralized their business units which now operate like individual, independent businesses. In each one, the division or department head acts like the CEO of his or her own business. Within smaller business units, you assume more responsibilities to make the business successful. Each member of the team is expected to add value to the organization. Added value comes from serving internal and external clients better, cutting costs, and increasing productivity.

It's now possible to disseminate information quickly, easily, and widely, so employees at every level in an organization now have access to critical information from the computers at their desks, wherever their desks may be!

Computers and telephones link people as never before, changing our ideas about where work must be done. Today, we have virtual work teams with members located in different buildings, cities, states, or even other countries who are linked by telecommunication networks. Some employees rarely trek into an office; they telecommute from their homes instead.

More companies are creating partnerships with other companies and with their external customers. The theme of partnership reaches into every aspect of the organization and filters down to every level. Divisions partner with other divisions; departments partner with other departments. This new way of doing business emphasizes the need for cooperation and collaboration.

Change occurs constantly and at an accelerating rate. The increased pace of progress means that your thinking must speed up as well. Psychologically, you must embrace the changes that technology makes possible and adjust to a workplace that is in a constant state of flux.

New Rules and Core Competencies

Changes in business have created new rules for survival and success. I've heard these rules reiterated by managers as they talk about what they want from their employees, and I've heard them repeated by employees describing the problems they experience in the workplace.

I have distilled the key qualities that companies and managers expect from their employees into what are called *core competencies*. They represent the critical skills and attributes you must have for success, whatever your job or industry. Core competencies include the following:

1. A tolerance for and an ability to manage change. This includes flexibility, resiliency, and an ability to handle stress.
2. An entrepreneurial attitude. This includes the willingness to take risks, make decisions independently and assertively, and assume ownership of problems.
3. Collaboration and teamwork skills. This includes interpersonal and communication skills.

4. Optimism and a can-do attitude.

5. Career self-management skills.

These core competencies intertwine, as I'll explain shortly. Weaving through them all is self-confidence, and what psychologist Daniel Golman calls "emotional intelligence." In his book of the same name, Golman writes that emotional intelligence includes self-motivation in the face of frustration, having control over moods and emotions, controlling impulses, delaying gratification, being empathetic to others, and keeping distress from swamping the ability to think.

In my opinion, core competencies are about personal skills, not technical skills. Managers sometimes focus only on the technical skills when hiring, and overlook the importance of these personal competencies. Big mistake! This omission can be costly. For example, someone hired for his technical skills who lacks the flexibility to work with different kinds of people may end up costing the company more that he's worth in personnel conflicts.

The Meaning of Core Competencies

I want to tell you more about what each core competency means because these competencies are the foundation for creating your successful career.

> *#1—A tolerance for and an ability to manage change; flexibility, resiliency, and an ability to handle stress.*

Companies look for a high tolerance for change. With change as a constant, you have to be skilled at adapting to it and coping with it if you are to succeed.

The same thing goes for the company itself. It is no longer enough just to have the best product. Nowadays a company must get that great product to market first. Companies that thrive manage change better than their competitors. Accordingly, they need people who manage change and adapt quickly. The pace of change and the pace of work have speeded up, so you have to speed up, too. As the old saying goes, if you snooze, you lose.

The old belief is that it is management's job to manage change. Now it's *your* job. Management lays out the big picture, but then it's your job to turn that concept into reality and make it come together.

In *Sacred Cows Make the Best Burgers*, Robert Kriegel and David Brandt list seven traits for what they call "change readiness." The traits are:

- Resourcefulness
- Optimism
- Adventurousness
- Drive
- Adaptability
- Confidence
- Tolerance for ambiguity

If you possess these traits, you're in a good position to handle change. The successful person is a change master, which is someone who can let go of old habits and outdated skills, beliefs, and ways of thinking, and who knows how to learn and adapt to new ways. A change master also knows how to handle the psychological transition that change brings.

In his book *Transitions*, William Bridges describes a change as a shift in external conditions that is relatively quick. A transition is an internal shift and is gradual. A transition takes place inside you in response to a change. Managing both change and transition are keys to success.

Outdated, pessimistic beliefs about change, such as "change is bad" and "change brings nothing but problems," will hold you back. Such beliefs can trap you and make you feel helpless, a victim of change. Positive, optimistic beliefs, such as "change is normal," "change brings opportunities and new possibilities," and "I can handle change," empower you to manage change successfully.

Successful change management requires you to handle ambiguity and uncertainty. These days we often have no clear answers. You need to improvise because it's frequently impossible to predict what is going to happen next. Coping with change requires being flexible and resilient, and knowing how to manage stress.

Flexibility

As changes alter the nature of work, jobs are not as clearly defined as they used to be. You're likely finding that you have more short-term assignments and that assignments change more quickly. This requires you to be flexible enough to handle several tasks simultaneously, to switch gears rapidly, and to move from one task to another, even from one job to another. Your thinking also needs to be flexible. Think like Indiana Jones in an action-packed thriller. See all aspects of a situation—the treasures and the perils—and consider all viewpoints instead of a hasty *yes* or *no*.

Resiliency

Managing change requires the ability to rebound quickly following mistakes, disappointments, and defeats. Your favorite movie characters most likely are *not* the ones who wallow in anger, depression or, when their situations change, self-pity. Remember Scarlett O'Hara in *Gone With the Wind*. Despite the dramatic changes in her life after the Civil War, she never dwelled on her losses.

Scarlett was resilient. Resiliency comes from optimistic thinking, another core competency that I address below. Optimistic thinkers learn from mistakes and don't dwell on disappointments. They perceive of failures as pushing them that much closer to eventual success. They move on. As Scarlett said, "Tomorrow is another day."

I hope you let go of this old (yet still popular) myth about change: "After this, things will settle down and get back to normal." What is normal, anyway? Constant change is normal now. There is no going back to the way it used to be. Dwelling on the past will only frustrate you and create more stress. Who needs that?

Successfully Managing Stress

Most stress is created when you try to control something out of your control. You can't control many changes that happen around you at work, but you can control your reactions to them. As a Chinese philosopher once said, "Peace is the mental condition in which you have accepted the worst." Many people create tremendous stress for themselves by wasting tons of energy resisting change. It would be far better—and certainly far healthier—to accept what is beyond your control and invest your energy positively in adapting to the changes.

People good at managing stress know it's important to keep a vibrant sense of humor. Ever notice how great movie characters say funny things during moments of high stress? Directors and scriptwriters know that humor can break tension and relieve stress. People good at managing stress also stay fit by eating right, getting enough sleep, and exercising to relieve tension. They also distance themselves from the gossips at work. Usually the biggest gossips are the most negative people; they are like emotional vampires. Sharing in their negativity only drains your enthusiasm and creates unnecessary stress.

#2—An entrepreneurial attitude; willingness to take risks, make decisions independently and assertively, and assume ownership of problems.

Restructuring and downsizings create smaller organizations, and everyone in the leaner group has a greater role to play in fostering success. How do you add value to your organization? Added value comes from serving both internal and external clients better, cutting costs, and increasing productivity.

As your responsibilities increase, you need to adopt an entrepreneurial outlook. This is a far more independent way of thinking and operating than you may be used to. It means pulling yourself out of the narrow confines of "This is my job." Rather, it is thinking, "This is my team, my department, my company. What can I do to make it successful?"

What Is Your Job?

I had a recent experience that illustrates the old "this is my job" belief. I stopped at a little café to grab some coffee to go. I looked around the busy room and saw that the waitress was occupied with customers at one of the tables. A young woman stood idly by the cash register. "I'd like a cup of coffee to go, please," I said to her.

She pointed to the waitress and said, "You'll have to ask the waitress for that." I explained I was in a hurry and the waitress was busy serving others. Unmoved, the cashier shrugged, "I'm the cashier. It's not my job to get coffee."

I wondered what she would have said had she been the café owner. Granted, the café wouldn't go out of business if I didn't get my coffee; but as a career coach, I thought to myself, "Is your job just to stand in front of the cash register? Wouldn't you help the whole business more if you served the customer?"

To check what your attitude toward your work is, take a moment to think about these questions. What is your job? How, specifically, do you contribute to helping your company achieve its goals?

An Entrepreneurial Attitude

I associate several characteristics with an entrepreneurial attitude.
- Creative thinking. Entrepreneurs are always looking for new ways to do things.
- Innovation. An innovative person is willing to take risks.
- Accountability. Entrepreneurs take responsibility for solving problems and making their business successful.
- Commitment. You must be fully committed to your work and to creating success.

Businesses large and small seek people with these entrepreneurial attributes. Every company wants to find newer, faster, cheaper, and better ways to succeed. Every company needs employees willing to handle the challenges and problems of the business. "The people who get on in this world," said George Bernard Shaw, "are the people who get up and look for the circumstances they want, and if they can't find them, make them."

Be a Risk-taker

No entrepreneur succeeds without taking risks. Of course, there's a difference between intelligent, thoughtful risks that push you forward, and reckless risk-taking. You may fear taking risks because you fear failing or making mistakes. However, we learn valuable lessons through experimenting, even from making mistakes. Sometimes the only way to find out what works is to find out first what doesn't work. Be sure you discuss with your manager the risks you plan to take so there's no misunderstanding about what you intend to accomplish and why.

Own the Problem

Some people think owning the problem means taking blame for it. By owning problems, I mean taking responsibility for solving problems, rather than ascribing blame. Successful people seek ways to fix problems rather than just pointing problems out or wasting energy complaining.

Peter Senge, author of *The Fifth Discipline: The Art and Practice of the Learning Organization,* stresses the need to apply a systems-thinking approach to addressing problems. Too often, we blame our problems on outside factors, claiming it's someone else's fault or shrugging and claiming that our organization prevents us from resolving the problem. If you use systems thinking, you'll recognize that there is no *outside* or *inside* and no *them* or *us.* We're all part of the same system. This approach helps get to the root cause of problems and create a solution.

Owning a problem means using independent, assertive decision-making skills. Rather than passing all decisions up to a higher level, step up to the situation, assess it, then act in the best interests of your team and company.

Commitment

Just as entrepreneurs commit to the success of their company, you need to commit likewise to your organization. You do this by committing to doing the best job you can do and being the best employee you can be.

This is as much about your own success as the company's. When you're fully committed, work is more satisfying and your productivity increases. In turn, you feel better about yourself. When your self-esteem increases, your self-confidence soars. High self-confidence feeds directly into feeling successful, and success breeds more success. Your reputation within your organization is enhanced. You create a winning formula for yourself as well as for your organization.

To be fully committed to your job, you must be in present time. This means that when you are working, you are completely there. You aren't thinking about unresolved issues from the past; you aren't projecting into the future. You aren't distracted by problems outside of work, either. You focus your energy into a laser beam of productivity.

By contrast, some people protest that they can't commit fully to their jobs because they are constantly distracted by personal issues. We all have an occasional crisis that diverts attention from work temporarily, yet some people create a lifestyle out of making excuses. If these people were in business for themselves, they'd never succeed. Their movie would be called *My Pathetic and Disastrous Career.*

#3—Collaboration and teamwork skills, including interpersonal and communication skills.

A team is a group of people working to complete a specific project within a particular time frame. A team is also a department where individuals work together to meet ongoing goals.

Technology enables virtual teams to meet through computer networks or videoconferencing links. Whether working with people face-to-face or through a computer, you want to build everyone's skills and knowledge to ensure that the team adds value. To do this, collaboration, cooperation, and clear communication—good people skills—are essential.

These are not new skills; they have always helped people succeed in the workplace. Today, however, it's critical to apply these skills when working with people of diverse backgrounds and mindsets. Recognize that each person brings a unique belief system to the table. Misunderstandings arise when you assume everyone shares your belief system. Flexibility, which I mentioned earlier, also applies here; you need to be flexible in expanding your mind to consider and respect other points of view.

In the most effective teams, members share these elements:
- Commitment to the team's success and to each individual's success
- A welcoming attitude to other team members on your own turf
- Willingness to confront difficult issues

Commitment to the Team's Success and to Individual Success

Commitment to a job, mentioned earlier, also applies to teams. It pays handsomely to recognize how your own individual success and your team's success are linked. No one works in isolation these days. Even if you are responsible for a discrete piece of a project, eventually your piece has to fit into the bigger picture, which is the team goal. Think beyond your own needs and consider the needs of everyone else on the team.

A Welcoming Attitude Toward Other Team Members On Your Turf

In order to commit to the team's success and welcome members onto your own turf, issues of competition must be addressed. While it's not wrong to be competitive, competition is often misplaced. Instead of competing *against* your team members, you should be competing *with* your team members to make your company more successful in the marketplace.

Welcoming others on your turf involves collaboration, sharing, trust, and respect. Some people become very territorial with knowledge and information. In a quest for self-glory, or a desire not to support a team member perceived as a rival, some people even withhold information needed by other team members in order to get their work done. If you do this, you risk sabotaging your team's —and ultimately your own—success.

Willingness to Confront Difficult Issues

Often problems that arise can be traced back to assumptions about expectations, project scope, and definition. For effective collaboration on a project, everyone involved needs to work with the same information. As you begin to work as a team, be sure to clarify and agree on the scope of the work, the tasks, and the deadlines, and confirm that everyone shares the same expectations.

Misunderstandings or problems are inevitable. As a team member, you have a responsibility to confront difficult issues and resolve them. Don't let them fester.

The wrong way to handle problems is to complain to other co-workers about the trouble you are having with someone. For best results, address the problem directly with the person you're having trouble with, and do it in an honest and respectful fashion.

#4—Optimism and a Can-do Attitude

Virtually every book about peak performance and success in life stresses the importance of an optimistic attitude. The power of positive thinking is essential. It made Jack, the Leonardo DiCaprio character in *Titanic*, an infectiously appealing person whose charm opened doors for him to socialize with wealthy first-class passengers. Facing overwhelming odds during the tragic sinking, he never let go of his heroic optimism, and he saved his love Rose's life with it. You may never ride a sinking ocean liner into the frigid North Atlantic, but your optimism can still open doors for you. That outlook is so important to success that I consider it a core competency.

Optimism directly links to self-confidence. Optimistic people expect to do well in their jobs even in the face of adversity. Their expectation fills them with the confidence to succeed.

Optimism interweaves among all the core competencies. In change management, a positive attitude makes adjusting to change easier. Those who think pessimistically just fight and struggle. Optimists approach change as opportunity and adventure. In the entrepreneurial attitude, your positive outlook says you are willing to take risks, make decisions, and approach problems creatively. Optimists consider mistakes and failed experiments as learning opportunities.

In a team setting, a positive attitude enhances collaboration and cooperation. Saying "I can," and "Let's give it a try" instead of "I can't," and "It'll never fly" bolsters team morale and keeps the focus on producing results. Meanwhile, a positive attitude makes managing your own career direction an exciting endeavor instead of a scary or dreary ordeal.

#5—Career Management Skills

In your movie, *My Successful Career*, you take responsibility for managing your future. Don't wait until your job has been eliminated to assess where your career is heading. Instead, understand that you are in charge of your career mobility right now. You determine your own career destiny. By taking a proactive stance now, you won't be the victim of change in the workplace.

Companies used to lay out career paths to move people up the ladder. As your own career hero, you need to uncover the opportunities creatively. As organizations have eliminated some layers of management, the ladder is less steep now, and you may find more opportunities through lateral moves. Opportunities may also lie in other companies, even other industries. People move more often from one job to another; it no longer is a warning sign on your résumé to show many different employers in your history.

Begin to take charge of your career by clarifying what you want to do and what kind of job environment suits you. Be true to yourself and decide what you really want. *What Color Is Your Parachute?* by Richard Nelson Bolles is a wonderful resource for walking you through this assessment phase.

Next, determine what skills you possess and what the marketplace is looking for. Think of yourself as being in business for yourself. If you were a self-employed consultant or an external vendor contracted for specific tasks, what skills, knowledge, and abilities would you bring? What needs does the company have? What would you need to learn or acquire to supply those needs?

The career assessment process continues throughout your entire career. Successful career management involves periodically reviewing your career goals, which will change as priorities in your life change.

Continuous self-development is another critical component in managing your career. Learning doesn't cease when you get a job. In today's world, skills and knowledge can become outdated at breakneck speeds. Be creative about your sources for learning. Classes, seminars, books, and tapes are traditional ways to learn, but explore different venues as well. Here are some suggestions:

- Join a professional organization to meet others in your field and to exchange information.
- Stay current with business trends by reading business magazines, trade journals, and the business section of your local newspaper.
- Cross-training or making a lateral move within your company is a good way to learn about other aspects of the business and to acquire new skills. Volunteer for new assignments or committees at work.
- Consider doing projects on your own time for charities. You can learn valuable skills this way that may lead directly to a future job.

Employment Myths

In his book *JobShift*, William Bridges writes about expectations and personal "rules" that hinder someone's ability to find work in a changing environment. I call these "myths"—they may have been true once upon a time, but not today. They all feed into beliefs that deny the active role you must play today in managing your career. If you believe these myths, you'll struggle to manage your career and respond to a changing work environment.

One myth Bridges cites says that if you're in the "right business," you have a secure job future. But what's the right business? Even in the computer industry, which many people consider the right business, organizations change constantly. Just being in the business is not enough—your skills and knowledge are constantly in danger of being outmoded by the next great technological breakthrough.

A related myth holds that some jobs in an organization will always be secure. I've heard innumerable laments from workers who believed their jobs were safe, only to wake up jobless when the company restructured, shifted priorities, or was sold. Safe and secure employment doesn't come from the "right business" or the "right job." It comes from knowing your skills, being alert to opportunities, and knowing how to market your skills to the companies that need them.

Another myth is that "good people" will always have a job. Don't rest on your laurels. The truth is that you can't rely on your past reputation to find—or to keep—a job. At whatever level you work in an organization, you must add value and continue helping the organization achieve its goals.

One final myth Bridges cites is that you shouldn't change careers past age forty. I'm not sure exactly where this myth originated. I've seen many people who left their corporate jobs in their forties or fifties and started their own businesses. Career management and career growth are not just for younger workers. Opportunities abound to grow and move, even into a completely different field or industry. The only thing holding you back from snatching an opportunity is your own mind. You can do whatever you set your mind to do.

Managers Also Have to Shift

The new work order means changes for managers, too. If you are a manager, look closely at the behavior you reward in the workplace. If you give a high performance rating to someone who brings projects in on time yet whose abrasive behavior frustrates other team members, you are rewarding

Identify Your Core Competencies

Look again at the list of core competencies required to succeed in the workplace. Take a moment to rate yourself by answering the following questions.

- Which competencies do you already possess? In which do you excel?
- Which competencies do you need to develop?
- How confident are you about your ability to develop these competencies?
- What, if anything, might make it difficult for you to develop these competencies?
- What will help you develop these competencies?

productivity at the expense of team harmony. You reinforce this behavior and teach other employees to imitate it.

New Beliefs for a New Workplace

As you prepare for your role in *My Successful Career*, the metaphorical movie of your working life, remember that you are living during a time of great social and technological transformation. Clinging to outdated beliefs about work is a sure road to nowhere. We have to replace antiquated beliefs with thinking that aligns with today's business needs and the core competencies.

As you read the section on core competencies, and if you completed exercise 2-A, you may have begun to recognize that your old, outdated beliefs can prevent you from developing the core competencies that lead to success. Perhaps you have already identified new beliefs you think you should embrace.

In this section, I want to present you with a set of new beliefs that form the foundation for creating a script for your successful career. These new beliefs will help you develop a positive, solution-oriented philosophy. All of these beliefs relate directly to the core competencies. Once you have read through this section, exercise 2-B on page 50 will help you assess to what extent you already hold these new beliefs.

> OLD BELIEF: **Change is to be avoided. Change is another word for *loss*.**
> NEW BELIEF: **Change is exciting. Change is another word for *opportunity*.**

We must change the sabotaging beliefs about change! This relates directly to the core competency of managing change. The old mindset poses change as something to fear—it's nothing but trouble; and if you wait, hunkered down with your head in the sand, things will revert to how they were. True, change does involve loss—such as the loss of familiar ways of doing things, comfortable relationships, perhaps status or even a job—but it also presents opportunities to grow and achieve success. Embrace change and look for the opportunities.

> OLD BELIEF: **Mistakes and failures are disasters.**
> NEW BELIEF: **Mistakes and failures are learning experiences.**

The old belief discourages risk-taking, stifles creativity, and limits the opportunities to learn and improve. Organizations that reinforce the old belief by punishing people who make mistakes are losing market position to companies that encourage risk-taking and innovation. Organizations need to adopt the new belief if they are to survive in today's competitive world. You also need to embrace the new belief if you are to be successful. The new belief frees you to explore, to change, and to grow. This new belief supports the core competencies of entrepreneurialism and an optimistic, can-do attitude.

> OLD BELIEF: **What can you do for me?**
> NEW BELIEF: **What can I do for myself?**

This old belief reflects dependency and passivity. However, you can't shift your dependency needs on to an organization. You may look to your manager for guidance and support, but you are in charge of your own performance.

The new belief is about being independent, taking an active, assertive posture, and taking responsibility for making things happen yourself instead of waiting for others. This new belief, and the next two that follow, underpin the core competency of having an entrepreneurial attitude.

> *OLD BELIEF:* **Look for something or someone to blame when a problem occurs.**
> *NEW BELIEF:* **Take responsibility for solving problems—even problems I didn't create.**

The old belief—another that reflects dependency—is about assigning blame, not about fixing problems. The idea that it is management's responsibility to fix things is old thinking. The new belief is about ownership, being accountable, taking responsibility and being solution-oriented. Don't use your energy to complain and finger-point; use it to fix things and make them better. If you see problems, don't simply inform your manager; instead, present your solutions and recommendations for solving the problems.

> *OLD BELIEF:* **Wait for "them" to decide and tell me what to do.**
> *NEW BELIEF:* **See what needs to be done. Make decisions and take action based on the facts known at present.**

Many people think management has all the answers. The truth is that you have answers, too. In fact, you probably know more about what is needed in your area of responsibility than management does. The new belief reflects the entrepreneurial attitude. Instead of waiting for your manager to tell you what to do, take the initiative, and do what needs to be done to make the organization successful.

> *OLD BELIEF:* **Identify with a job title.**
> *NEW BELIEF:* **Identify with a team for which everyone works toward the same set of goals.**

Many people confuse their job title with their identity, like the young woman in the café who said, "I am a cashier." Doing this focuses only on performing the tasks in your job description with no consideration for how your actions contribute to the organization's goals. Some managers perpetuate this thinking when they tell employees, "You just concentrate on what you're supposed to do and let me worry about the big stuff." Identifying beyond your job title means contributing to the team effort; it frequently encourages cross-training that adds to your skill set. This new belief and the one that follows relate to the core competency of collaboration and teamwork.

> OLD BELIEF: **It's not my job.**
> NEW BELIEF: **I'll pitch in where I can.**

The old belief limits your responsibility, reduces participation, and creates feelings of isolation. Imagine a second baseman and shortstop arguing about who should dive for the grounder: "Yo, that's not my department!" Instead, both players go after the ball because both have a stake in the outcome; both are focused on the team goal of winning the game. In today's workplace, success requires removing the focus from "What is my job?" and applying it to "What is it that needs to be done?" Thinking in this broader way also shows you how your actions beyond the boundaries of your job can have an impact on the company's success.

> OLD BELIEF: **Ask "Why?"**
> NEW BELIEF: **Ask "Why not?"**

The old belief is an excuse to resist change. "Why?" comes from a defensive and self-protective posture when you are feeling threatened by change or by other people's way of doing things. Saying "Why not?" breaks down the defensive posture, reframes the situation, and opens your mind to other options, new opportunities, and new possibilities. The new belief reflects an entrepreneurial mindset, as well as the optimistic, can-do attitude that are two of the core competencies.

The following four beliefs relate to the core competency of career self-management skills.

> OLD BELIEF: **Security comes from loyalty to your company.**
> NEW BELIEF: **Security comes from having skills that are needed in the marketplace.**

If you have been laid off or told your job is being eliminated, you've had first-hand experience with the destruction of this old belief. Showing up faithfully day after day is no longer enough. Now you must bring to the table the skills and attitudes employers need. This means you must take an active role in identifying and acquiring those skills and attitudes and updating them as employers' needs change. The new belief redefines security and recognizes that you create your own security; a company does not bestow it on you.

> *Old Belief* : **There is no need to continue one's education after getting a job.**
> *New Belief*: **Life involves continuous learning and retraining.**

This new belief ties into the previous new belief about job security. You educate yourself to *get* a job; you must continue to educate yourself to *keep* a job. Education is a life-long process; it is more important now than ever before because your skills will become obsolete if you don't stay current. People often date themselves not by their age, but by their unwillingness to keep learning and growing.

> *Old Belief*: **I am an employee. My current job is the only option and there are no choices.**
> *New Belief*: **I am employable. My current job is my choice and is one of many options I have.**

Shifting from old to new beliefs represents taking the responsibility to make yourself attractive to employers by acquiring the skills, knowledge, and competencies they want. In his book *JobShift*, author William Bridges suggests taking this one step further and thinking of yourself as an employer, the CEO of a company called "You & Company." Being employable means you know the essence of your contribution counts, not the number of hours you have logged or how busy you are.

> *Old Belief*: **The company is responsible for its employees' future.**
> *New Belief*: **I determine my future.**

The old belief reflects helplessness and a dependency on others. The people who cling to this belief are abdicating responsibility for managing their careers. Sometimes they then blame the company, or feel victimized or betrayed, if their careers do not progress as they had hoped. The new belief reflects empowerment and being in charge of your career and your vision of your future. Your manager may advise you or support your career goals, but you have to be the active director of your career.

It is a mistake to think that the core competencies and new beliefs apply only to people who work in corporations. They apply to people everywhere in all industries and in companies of every size. It is not the size of the organization that determines success; it's the people who are in it.

Defining Success

When I talk about being successful in the workplace, many things come to mind. I have my own ways of defining success, and you also need to decide for yourself how you define and measure it. Promotions and monetary rewards are two traditional measurements, but they are not the only ways. Here are some of the ways I define success:

- Liking your job and enjoying being at work.
- Achieving the goals you set for yourself.
- Responding to changes with confidence and eagerness.
- Getting projects done without undue stress.
- Tackling unpleasant tasks without procrastinating.
- Having good relationships with your co-workers and boss.
- Feeling good about your contributions and job accomplishments.
- Seeking new opportunities to learn and grow.
- Having balance in your life— both a fulfilling work life and a satisfying personal life outside of work.
- Seeing yourself as a competent, capable and successful person.
- Feeling positive about yourself and your future.

Sometimes you can't be as successful at work as you want because you're not in the right place. Your values and goals are not in accord with those of the organization. You need to be truthful with yourself about why you're struggling. You may think, "The rules in this company are unfair; they say I have to do this . . . ." In truth, it may be that the rules *are* fair but you don't want to follow orders or policies because they greatly conflict with your personal values. Maybe you simply don't like to follow anyone else's rules. You'll feel un-

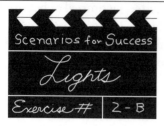

Identify Your New Beliefs

Refer to the beliefs you identified in chapter one for exercise 1-A on pages 13 and 14, and exercise 1-B on page 18. Which beliefs are outdated for today's workplace? Which do you need to let go of in order to put your new beliefs in place? All the new beliefs are listed here for you to think about as you answer the questions below.

- Change is exciting. Change is another word for *opportunity*.
- Mistakes and failures are learning experiences.
- What can I do for myself?
- I take responsibility for solving problems—even problems I didn't create.
- See what needs to be done. Make decisions and take action based on the facts known at present.
- Identify with a team for which everyone works toward the same set of goals.
- I'll pitch in where I can.
- Ask "Why not?"
- Security comes from having skills needed in the marketplace.
- Life involves continuous learning and retraining.
- I am employable. My current job is my choice and is one of many options I have.
- I determine my future.

1. Which new beliefs do you already possess?
2. Which new beliefs do you need to put in place?
3. Which old beliefs do you need to change?
4. What, if anything, might make it difficult for you to change your old beliefs?

happy and frustrated if your values are not in alignment with your company's values. If your job, the work environment, and the company are not the right places for you—and they may not be—it could be time to end the struggle and move on instead.

No Such Thing as a Perfect Job

Some of us spend a lot of time searching for perfection in our jobs and being disappointed when we can't find it. We may have unrealistic notions of how a job should be or what a job should give. You may be upset that you're not making as much money as you want, or that you don't have the status you would like. Maybe a different job would give you more of what you want. You have to be realistic, however; no job will give you *everything* you desire. Changing jobs can post some gains, but it may also result in some losses.

Reassess what is important for you in a job; see if your current job provides enough of what you want. If you are getting the things that matter most to you, such as recognition from others, good working relationships, and interesting assignments, maybe you can let go of perfection. Instead, go for quality. Value the things you have that are important to you and let go of the unrealistic childhood notion that you can have everything.

I'll Take a Pound of Self-Esteem, Please

Many people tell me their low self-esteem holds them back from being successful. They believe that they would be successful if they had high self-esteem, as if it were a pill they could pick up at the drug store. Obviously, it isn't. Nor is it something you can acquire by repeating positive affirmations such as "I am a worthy person" or "I am competent at my job." Self-esteem is not endowed by others. You get it from your positive experiences, your successes, and from the good feelings you have about what you do with your life. Creating success boosts self-esteem because it is a result of your actions and feelings.

I hear clients say, "I just want to be happy in my job." Happiness, like self-esteem and self-confidence, is not something you *get*. It's something that comes to you as a result of your actions. Happiness and satisfaction are by-products of your experiences and successes. You feel happy when you are using the skills you enjoy. You feel happy when your values and goals are in alignment with your company's values and goals.

How Do You Define Success?

What is your idea of success at work? This must be your own vision, not the vision of other people. Since your vision of success can change depending on what's going on in your life, events in your personal life can affect your vision of success at work. Reaching certain milestones—such as having children, turning forty, fifty, or sixty, or losing a job—may make you reassess your life, the role of work in your life, and your ideas about success. Exercise 2-C gives you the opportunity to define your ideas about success at work.

Success at work means shedding your old scripts from other movies you may have starred in and letting go of the beliefs that no longer fit in today's workplace. In the next chapter we'll look at how to do this to prepare you for your winning performance in *My Successful Career.*

Defining Success

Scenarios for Success
Lights
Exercise # | 2 - C

Take a moment right now to define success for yourself by answering the following questions. Be as specific as you can.

- What would success look like for you in your current job?
- What things would you like to do or change at work that would increase your feelings of success?
- What do you think you will gain by being successful on your own terms?
- What would you lose by being successful on your own terms?
- What holds you back from being as successful as you want to be?

Chapter 3

Character Development
Spotlighting Your Motivation

As an actor in the future blockbuster *My Successful Career,* one of your jobs is to fully develop the leading character—*you!* In a movie production, the writer, director, and actors all need to understand what drives the individual characters to think the way they think and act the way they act. In our moviemaking metaphor, you are the writer, director, and actor of your life, so you need to understand yourself if you want to turn your life into a winning production.

In this chapter, we will look at your character development, which in this case means what your workplace personality is like. We'll look at what motivates you. This book is about becoming successful, and most people I coach suffer from feelings of work-related failure, believing they have missed out on fulfilling their dreams. First we'll focus on the thinking and acting habits that don't breed success—that in fact compound one's misery—and then we'll get to the business of claiming your power and releasing the misery.

Who Wrote This Miserable Script?
I get a litany of reasons when I ask my clients, "What prevents you from being as successful at work as you'd like to be?"
- My boss is unreasonable.
- The company won't let me succeed.
- My co-workers dislike me.

- My spouse doesn't support me.
- My kids need me.
- I'm too old.
- I'm too young.
- I don't have the skills.
- I can't learn new things.
- People don't like me because I'm different (race, culture, weight, age, religion, sexual orientation).

My clients tend to point the finger of blame at another person or thing. Have you used any of the reasons above to explain your frustration or unhappiness? If you won't admit to using them, have they crossed your mind, even if just for a second or two?

Many of us are conditioned to look outside of ourselves to find something to blame for our problems. Naturally, this world is filled with unreasonable bosses, frustrating company rules, nonsupportive spouses, and demanding children. We also find the planet overrun with racism, sexism, ageism, and other forms of discrimination. While these are very real problems—both in and out of the workplace—that can have a definite impact on success, you can still tackle and overcome them.

Recognize the Part You Play

As I listen to my clients talk about their job situations, I often feel as if I am a script editor looking at the conflicts in their stories. The main character very often creates his own torment. The truth is that the world *does* bubble and boil with mean and nasty conflicts that we could use to explain why we are stuck where we are. It's also true that it's easier—and some would argue more fun—to blame other people or other things for our problems than to peer inside our mind to see how we may be creating our own conflicts. *I contend that you are responsible for most of the problems you have! You create most of your own problems by the way you react to life's events.*

Feeling a little faint? Or angry? Feel like throwing the book across the room? This is not an easy concept to swallow. In fact, if those last two sentences in the previous paragraph didn't stir up some emotional froth, check them out one more time: *I contend that you are responsible for most of the problems you have! You create most of your own problems by the way you react to life's events.*

Does this sound crazy? It's actually good news! If I can show you that you may be the source of your own difficulties, I can also show you that you have more control over your problems than you ever thought. No one is denying your emotions or your pain. Rather, I am telling you the truth as I see it, and as I've seen it with thousands of clients. As you accept responsibility for your problems, you immediately begin to counter with solutions, and you can really start improving your work life.

Here's a truth: Nothing changes when you blame others for the problems you're having! About the best you can expect is momentary relief, and there's very little satisfaction in that. Blaming others doesn't take away the misery. Your success will be a much more meaningful victory when you take responsibility for your part in any scene.

One reason why my movie-making metaphor is so powerful is that when you look at your career as the film *My Successful Career*, you can see the role you play in creating your life. How would you feel if your life were projected on a huge movie screen for all the world to see? Would you like watching how you designed your life? Would you admire the main character?

You star in every scene in every plot in your life. No one is passive in his or her personal script. Life doesn't just happen. In each scene, you choose what you do or don't do, even what you think and feel. You may sit in a meeting and say nothing and do nothing. A film director could show the essence of your presence on screen. He might show you not speaking, quietly observing others with your eyes. Perhaps you don't make eye contact with anyone at all, but focus your eyes on the notepad in front of you. Even when you think you are doing nothing in a scene from your life, you are actually doing something!

Most important, other people in the scene react to your choices. They will note, consciously or unconsciously, what you do during the meeting. Do you look at people who speak, or do you just stare ahead? If you remain silent when the meeting moderator asks for comments on an agenda item, the others in the scene will note, consciously or unconsciously, that you said nothing.

What you do at the meeting determines in part how others will respond to you afterwards. Maybe your personal style in meetings is quiet reflection. Maybe you want to be invisible at the meeting. Whatever your motive, your silence is noticed by others and has an impact on what they think and conclude about you. Someone may come up to you later and say, "You were so quiet, I wondered if something troubled you." Another person may avoid talking to you because he interpreted your silence as a lack of interest, aloofness, or your disagreement with the majority viewpoint.

Now expand this scene out to the rest of your life. You may think you do nothing to create problems for yourself; you may have logical, profound, even verifiable excuses for your problems. As the hero of your life movie, however, you need to get beyond that to overcome the perceived obstacles. You play a part in every scene in your life. Recognizing and owning up to that part is critical to achieving satisfaction.

Owning Your Life

You create your belief system and your thoughts, feelings, and behaviors; they don't just spring up inside your head, heart, and life fully formed. You author your script. Who else could own your beliefs, thoughts, feelings, and behaviors but you?

When people say things like, "This slow computer makes me so frustrated," or "Hearing about those policy changes really ticks me off," they're blaming an outside event. They're not acknowledging how their thinking has created their feelings. When people say, "He made me so angry," or "She humiliated me," they are empowering an outside person as the cause of their feelings. People who say, "I couldn't help it; I just had to say something," or "What else could I do but defend myself" are denying power and responsibility for their actions and the thinking that led to those actions.

Being an adult implies owning both your own life and the response to everything that happens in it. You usually are not dealt the hand you want, but you can always determine how you will play it. It's your script, and you can choose to rewrite it. Think like John Dunbar, the Kevin Costner character in *Dances with Wolves*, who went out to the prairies of frontier America. He found nothing in his job as a cavalry officer as he expected it would be, and he constantly had to rewrite the script of his life, for both his physical and his emotional survival.

No one's script is entirely ineffective. You will always have some things in your script that work well for you. Be sure to acknowledge these good parts as you note the things you want to change and improve.

When you own your script, recognize that you still have an internal child who wants to star in your scenes. This is the impulsive, pleasure-hungry, emotional part of you. If you don't acknowledge that child part occasionally, it can control you with emotional outbursts. The adult part of you is aware that you have options; it knows when it's okay to be childlike and when it's best to behave in an adult fashion appropriate to the situation. The adult mind, not the child mind, has the experience and sophistication to realize the impact that the choices you make have on you and others in the workplace.

Take Ownership For the Part You Play

Dwight's manager mentioned that some of Dwight's co-workers were unhappy with his habit of hoarding important information that they needed to get the job done. Dwight responded, "That's just the way I am." Granted, we all have individual styles of working. However, if you get feedback, as Dwight did, that your style affects others negatively, it's time to look at making some changes for the sake of cooperation.

Dwight's response really says that he's unwilling to consider changing. He's glued himself into an *I am this way* box as if he can't imagine acting any other way. He owns who he is, but he shows he has no concern about his team members and takes no responsibility for his inappropriate behaviors. That attitude doesn't cut it in the today's workplace. His resistance to change could well mean that the clock is ticking on his stay with the company.

If Dwight is to be successful at work, he must take ownership for his behavior. He might want to look at the script that causes him to behave as he does, including the part written by his ghostwriters. If he's unhappy with the movie of his life, he needs to rewrite the script.

Like Dwight, Eric also needs to look at his script and how he can rewrite it. As a child, Eric felt neglected and ignored by his parents. His mother resented getting pregnant with Eric because it interrupted her career. Unwittingly, she blamed Eric and took out her anger on him with sarcastic barbs. His father, a very successful executive, was seldom home, and when he was, he had little interest in spending time with Eric. An only child, Eric spent most of his time by himself, seeking refuge from his loneliness with a make-believe world populated with imaginary playmates. Eric grew up feeling that his parents would be happier if he had never been born.

These feelings stayed with him as he grew up, and now he projects his feelings about his parents onto other people. His belief that he does not matter to anyone keeps him from interacting much with others at work. He eats lunch at his desk rather than joining his co-workers who go to lunch together.

He chooses to attend group meetings by teleconference instead of walking one block to the conference room in another building in the business park.

It's true that Eric's parents neglected him. It's also true that he felt lonely and ignored as a child. It would have been nice if his parents had been more attentive; but as a working adult, Eric can't blame his parents for his loneliness and isolation today. He isolates himself with this thinking: "I'm not interesting enough for people to want me around." He reinforces these thoughts and feelings with his actions: when he chooses to eat lunch at his desk, he separates himself from his co-workers. When he opts to attend team meetings via telephone instead of in person, he isolates himself further.

Eric complains that he feels isolated, yet he does not see that he's creating his own problem by removing himself from others. He also does not see that he has a choice. He can stay where he is in his uncomfortable, though familiar, spot, or he can change his thinking, rewrite his script, and modify his behaviors. By making the second choice, Eric would feel better about himself and feel a sense of connection with his peers.

You Have a Choice

Sometimes situations at work leave you feeling angry, hurt, afraid, or humiliated. For example, a meeting takes place on a project you're involved with, yet you weren't invited to attend. Your boss might badger you every time something goes wrong, or a co-worker takes credit for your hard work. Perhaps you hear rumors of cutbacks coming to your department. Are you doomed to suffer and be miserable for your entire career? The answer is Yes!—if you want to be. The answer is also No!—if you don't want to be. You always have a choice. In fact, you have three choices:

1. You can do nothing and continue to feel miserable and frustrated.
2. You can try to change the situation.
3. You can change your reactions to the situation.

Choosing Not to Change is a Choice

You get to choose what you want to do. Do you realize that doing nothing and staying miserable is a choice? This choice not only leaves you suffering, but it may make several other people close to you suffer, too. You may not realize choosing to do nothing and remaining miserable can have a demoralizing impact on other people.

Always look for choices you can make. For example, in the situation where you weren't invited to the project meeting, you have several options:

- You can sit and fume about not being invited.
- You can fire off an angry e-mail message to the project team leader.
- You can call the team leader's manager and complain about what happened.
- You can tell several other people how angry you are.
- You can talk to the person in charge of issuing invitations to the meetings.

What other options can you think of? You need to determine which option will most likely get the results you really want, which in this case is an invitation to all future project meetings. The last option, talking to the person in charge of issuing invitations, is likely to be the best choice for getting that.

In talking with the person in charge of meeting invitations, you have more options. You decide how you'll communicate with that person. You could choose to suppress your anger, or you could choose to express it. If you choose to express it, you could then choose to throw a tantrum with shouting, hostility, and nasty words, or you could choose to use a matter-of-fact voice and say, "I was upset to find out I was not invited to the project meeting. I think I should be on the invitation list because I represent a group that will be affected by this project."

You always have the power to make a choice. Career success and happiness depend on making good choices.

Change the Situation

Rather than choosing to stay stuck in misery, you can choose to change the situation. You may be surprised when you find out how much power you have to change uncomfortable situations.

Paul and Hank, two men in Lisa's department, regularly told tasteless jokes at the weekly staff meeting. Lisa found their behavior obnoxious and the jokes offensive. She thought about her options. One option was just to walk out of the meeting. That wasn't practical because she might miss some important information, and her boss might misinterpret her leaving as disinterest in her work. Lisa next considered going to Human Resources to complain, but she decided that complaining might be perceived as making trouble.

It reminded her of her childhood, when she'd run to her mom to get her older brothers to stop teasing her. Lisa shifted to an adult mode and decided to talk directly to the two men.

Just before the next staff meeting, she spoke to them in private. "I'd appreciate it if you'd stop making off-color jokes at staff meetings. They make me uncomfortable." She explained briefly what she found offensive about the jokes. The two men looked at each other, then Paul said, "Okay, Lisa. No problem. We don't want to make you feel bad."

Twenty minutes into the meeting, Paul cracked a sexist joke that made Hank roar with laughter, and Lisa turn crimson with rage. Paul then glanced at Lisa and said, "Lisa, why aren't you laughing? Don't you get it?"

After the meeting, Lisa approached Paul and Hank and said, "I asked you to stop making those offensive jokes, and you said you would. The next time you do this, I'm going to confront you in front of everyone in the meeting."

"Hey, Lisa, lighten up," Hank said. "Paul was just teasing you. Can't you take a joke?"

"I'm serious," Lisa said evenly. "I'm warning you that your joking needs to stop."

At the next staff meeting, Paul and Hank refrained from cracking any jokes until the meeting was breaking up. Then as people rose to leave, Hank said, "We caved in to Lisa and promised her we wouldn't tell any more jokes at the staff meeting, but since we're done now, have you heard the one about the . . ." Before Hank had delivered the punch line, Lisa interrupted. "I told you I find your jokes offensive, and I've asked you twice to stop telling them, but you continue. Why is that?"

"Yeah, why is that?" Della piped in. "Why do you keep telling these nasty jokes?"

"They aren't even funny—they're just sick," Cora added.

"Okay, okay," Hank said. "We get it. No more jokes."

Della and Cora said in unison, "Good!"

"Thanks. I appreciate that," Lisa said, looking at both men. Rather than simmering in her anger, she exercised a proactive option. Her willingness to try to change the situation resulted in success and boosted her confidence. She learned that if she acted, she had the power to change things. If confronting the men directly had not worked, Lisa would have followed protocol and informed her manager.

Trying to change a situation often requires discussing issues with others. Some people would rather jump into a snakepit than do that. If the thought of asking for what you want or need terrifies you, be aware that you are *choosing* not to change the situation.

You may think that talking to another person about a problem is being confrontational. Confrontations usually happen when people wait until they are steaming mad before they say anything about what's bothering them. I advise you to speak to the other person before you reach your boiling point. This way, you can tell someone that their behavior is having a negative effect on you without confronting them. Think of it as educating the other person.

A common complaint around offices is that someone is playing a radio too loud. One client asked me, "Don't these people realize that their radio annoys others?" I'd like to give radio-players the benefit of the doubt and say, "No, they don't realize it." Like most of us, these people are thinking only about their own needs, their own life movie. They want a soundtrack in their movie; if no one complains, they don't realize other people prefer the golden sounds of silence.

If someone does something that bothers you, you should make that person aware of it. By backing away from discussing your irritation for fear that the person will attack you, you choose to stay stuck. You also risk escalating your anger until it erupts into a full-blown tirade, and when it reaches that point, you are likely to create the very confrontation you hoped to avoid.

It is especially critical to bring up for honest discussion any problems, concerns, or issues you have with another person in team situations. It's part of being a responsible and accountable team member. Too many people stay stuck in their helpless, powerless scripts and avoid such discussions. Even worse, they often complain to a third party, such as an uninvolved co-worker, rather than talking directly with the person who can resolve the issue. Backstabbing like this is all too common at work. If you handle upsetting situations by commiserating with an uninvolved co-worker, here is what the result may be:

- You may relieve your discomfort.
- You may gain sympathy and attention.
- You may enjoy gossiping with your co-worker.
- You did nothing to change the situation.
- You are part of the problem, and may add to the problem.

Should you *ever* talk to a co-worker about a problem with another co-worker? I advise doing this only if you respect his or her point of view and you believe you could benefit from that person's ideas about how best to raise your concerns directly. You also need to agree that this consultation is strictly professional and confidential, not to be repeated to other co-workers. The next step is to take charge and to be part of the solution.

Sometimes changing the situation involves thinking creatively. For example, Jackie was distressed to discover her name had been left off a telephone cost-reduction report that her team had written. She felt it was important for her career that the division managers who received the report knew she had been a contributor. Rather than feel sorry for herself or cursing the typist, she proactively sent an e-mail to the seven division managers. In her note, she wrote, "I am following up on the report we sent you describing ways to reduce company telephone costs. Along with Rex and Melvin, my teammates on this project, I am happy to answer any questions you may have about our recommendations." Her actions made her feel resourceful and drew extra attention to the report to boot.

Change How You React

Another strategy for handling stress in the workplace is to change your reactions to the situation. Believe it or not, this is where you truly have the most power and control.

The external situations in the workplace—who your boss is, company policies, other people's words and actions—are beyond your control. You can complain about company rules, but you probably have little real chance of changing them. You usually have little or no control over other people's behaviors, and trying to control other people most often leads to frustration.

You *do* have control over your internal life—your thoughts about the events that happen at work. You have control over your attitudes, behaviors, and beliefs about yourself and others. You can choose how to react to whatever happens to you. Here are four key points to remember:

- The only person you can control is you.
- The only actions or behaviors you can control are yours.
- The only thoughts, feelings, and reactions you can control are yours.
- You have the power to change your thoughts, feelings, and actions.

These four points are key to neutralizing your pain and misery. Once you live your life according to these four points, you'll be directing yourself in successful scripts for your career and your life.

You may already be familiar with the eternal wisdom of the twelve-step Serenity Prayer (attributed to both Fredrich Oetinger and Reinhold Neibuhr): *God grant me the serenity to accept the things I cannot change, the courage to change the things I can, and the wisdom to know the difference.*

Children have a raw response to events. When something happens, they react in a certain predictable way without a whole repertoire of responses. Children have little insight into themselves, and they don't realize there are multiple ways to perceive things. Adults, however, choose from a wide array of learned responses. You can create new responses that are more appropriate for the situation and for who you are as an adult. You can choose how you think about what's happened, how you feel, and how you act. You are in charge of your script.

Who is Poking Me?

"Can I really choose my reactions?" Yes, you can. Imagine this: you step into an elevator filled with people. Suddenly, you feel a sharp poke in your back. What is your reaction? Annoyance? Then you are poked again, more sharply this time. What's your reaction this time? Anger? As you turn around, ready to glare at the perpetrator, you see a blind person holding a cane. The handle of the cane has been poking you in the back. What's your reaction now? Still angry? Or did the anger melt to pity, perhaps even to embarrassment that you were so angry at someone clearly unaware of what happened.

You instantly changed your reaction once you reassessed the situation. You can learn how to invoke a similar mental process to change your reactions in other situations, including times when people are deliberately trying to aggravate you. Learning this skill helps keep you even-keeled at work, and once you feel the power it gives you, you'll like how that leaves you feeling better in all areas of your life. You'll see how you really are the director of your life.

Here's something to try for a day—or at least for several hours. Make the conscious choice to draw all your responses from a kind, generous place within you. What does this mean? Say that someone cuts in front of you on your commute. Try waving your hand while thinking, "It's OK. You must be in a big hurry." Try smiling at co-workers, even the grumpy ones. When co-workers are carrying on a loud conversation just a few feet from your desk, gently shush them and say, "Hey, guys, can you please keep it down in the work zone. I need to concentrate." Remember that you're educating them about your needs, not confronting them.

This may take some experimentation; it may be quite unlike you to be so positive, so forgiving, or so generous of spirit. You may think of it as weakness. Play with it as an acting role, as if you have just been signed by a Hollywood director to play the leading role in a new movie, *The Transformation of My Existence.* Even if you think you're playing a weird game of pretend, you may find that you soon feel more in control. You will likely find that your co-workers will respond to you much differently. Instead of paying the high price for old scripts that create misery, you begin to reap rewards for a new script that comes from a generous part of you.

Choosing Thoughts and Feelings

Vanessa and Lenore were colleagues as analysts in the compensation department. After they had worked together for two years as peers, a supervisory position opened up in the department for which both were eligible. Vanessa chose not to apply, while Lenore did apply and was hired for the position. At the same time, Lenore enrolled in an evening completion program at a local college and eventually finished her degree. A year later, her excellent performance as supervisor and her newly awarded degree earned her a promotion to vice president.

When the promotion was announced, Vanessa seethed. "I work just as hard as Lenore does. How come she got the title?" She decided that Lenore was "just an apple-polisher," and further thought, "Those VP titles are a dime a dozen. They give them to anybody." Vanessa's anger grew so intense that she found it difficult to congratulate Lenore and chat with her. At the same time, Vanessa felt guilty about her anger. Over the next week or so, she went home every night churned-up inside. She finally decided that she needed to deal with the situation by taking an honest look at what was going on inside herself.

Vanessa had several choices. She could do nothing and continue to feel terrible. But she knew her pain would just get worse unless she did something. As Vanessa pondered her plight, she realized that her anger masked feelings of envy. She was jealous of Lenore's new title and recognition. "I'd like to be a vice president, too," she thought. Then she recalled that she'd chosen not to pursue the supervisory opening the previous year. She still didn't want the pressures of being a supervisor, nor did she want to take on the extra workload involved in returning to school.

When Vanessa accepted her feelings about work and school, she realized that she had made choices and that these choices had consequences. Although she wanted a VP title, too, when she asked herself if she were willing to work as hard as Lenore to earn it, she honestly had to answer *no*. When she looked at it that way, Vanessa felt her envy dissipate.

Many people have experienced the jealousy and bitterness that Vanessa experienced. They want the promotion, status, or pay raise, but they are not willing to do what it takes to earn them. Instead, they choose to grouse and complain to others. While favoritism and unfairness exist, most of the time the people who get the rewards have worked for them.

When Leaving Is the Best Choice

I've worked with people who are in situations or jobs that are extremely uncomfortable or intolerable for them. They have tried to change things, but couldn't, or they have no power to make the required changes. They've tried changing their reactions, but that has not relieved their discomfort. In these cases, we have to consider another option: To choose to leave the situation and find another job. In some cases, that's the best choice.

Deborah was a human resources specialist for a large corporation. "I love my work, but I hate my job," she would say. She derived great satisfaction from helping people who came to her for advice or assistance, yet she was unhappy working in a company that valued profits over people. She knew she could never change the company's values and management practices. She also felt that changing her reaction to these practices was not realistic because her fundamental values were in basic conflict with the company's. She decided she could no longer afford the misery of staying where she was. To be true to her values, she resigned and found a similar job with a small start-up company where the company president said during the interview, "We believe that if you put people first, the profits will follow."

For Deborah, leaving was the best choice. It may be the best choice for you, too. If you strongly disagree with your company's beliefs, values, policies, or culture, consider finding a company with a mission and vision you can support. If you cannot respect the people you work with and the company's business practices frustrate you, your best choice may be to leave. When frustrated by the hierarchy in a large corporation, some people discover career happiness in a smaller company. Others think their small company has limited career options, and a larger company makes more sense. Some people don't like working for others, and their best choice may be to work on their own as an entrepreneur. You will be most successful in the environment that matches your needs and values.

At certain times in our lives, our personal situations change and necessitate a change in our work situation. Jake was a successful litigator on the partner track in a prestigious law firm. His wife, Susan, an equally successful financial advisor, had recently given birth to their second child. Unfortunately, the baby was born with medical problems that would require multiple surgeries during her first five years.

Jake's law firm required he carry a caseload that averaged a minimum of fifty hours a week. When Jake first came to see me, he was tormented by the conflict between his professional goals and his personal commitment to raise his two children with Susan. After a few sessions, he was able emotionally to let go of his dream of being a partner in the law firm and decide that a position with another organization would enable him to fulfill his personal commitment. He began to send out résumés and network with colleagues and friends, and he soon found a satisfying corporate legal position that gave him the time to tend to his family.

Don't just leap to another company as a quick problem fix, however. I call that the geographic solution. You will almost always find that your problems follow you since they are part of *you*, not part of the job or the company you left behind. Some people continually change jobs, hoping to find the perfect job, boss, or company. If your problems are replicated in the new organization, you can't blame the organization. You need to look at what's inside you and how you must change to be successful.

People tell me about horrible job situations and say that they can do nothing to change things. When I've asked if they've considered finding another job, they quickly respond, "Oh no, I could never leave." When I ask why not, they say they'll lose their great medical insurance or vacation benefits. Does that sounds familiar? What I always tell these people is: *You are choosing this. You are choosing financial benefits over happiness.*

In any job situation, you can always complain about how you're suffering. But when you're complaining, I want you to say to yourself, "I choose this." When you invoke *I choose,* you start to see that you have power. Once you acknowledge this power, you can write your own script for success. You can direct yourself toward the quality of the life you want to have.

Masking the Problem

Some people choose alcohol or drugs to block out unpleasant feelings or to try to make themselves feel better. When substance abusers are confronted at work with their poor performance, invariably they try to manipulate their managers. They deny, defend, rationalize, and minimize their behavior. They blame their problems on other people and other things. Their families and friends often believe that if these people stopped drinking or using drugs, all the problems would be solved, but abstinence is just the first step.

Substance abuse is often a symptom of a deeper unhappiness stemming from an inability to cope with one's thoughts and feelings. Other addictive behavior—such as eating disorders, gambling, or excessive spending that results in crippling credit card debt—can be just as damaging as substance abuse.

These addictions are very real problems in the workplace that need to be addressed. Acknowledging addictive, self-abusive behavior is a big step in taking ownership for the role you play in creating your problems. By all means, get yourself into a treatment program to stop the self-destructive behavior. Then, when you are on your way to recovery, start tackling the real problems you have been using alcohol, drugs, sex, food, or money to hide from.

People involved in twelve-step recovery programs learn that they can always choose to abstain from the addictive behavior one day at a time. Recovery programs can help you recognize the choices you make.

Playing the Victim . . . Oh, Poor Little Me

When we are in discomfort or distress, deep down we may wish someone would come along to rescue us and make it all better, just as our mother or father did when we were children. Even if we didn't have a rescuing mother or father, we may still yearn for someone to make things right to ease our misery. When we are in distress, even the strongest and most independent of us may feel out of control and helpless. That's when the rescue fantasy kicks in.

When a colleague of mine feels distressed, she mocks a baby's cry—"Waaah! Mommy!" It's her way of acknowledging the fantasy and letting go of it. Then she says, "Okay, now how do I fix this?" and turns the focus to problem solving.

Your rescue fantasy may be so satisfying and comforting, however, that you can't let go of it. Do you become the victim of every workplace plot you star in? Do you blame others for your miserable existence? Do you moan, "They did it to me?" Do you think you can be motivated and productive

on the job only if you work for someone who fits a certain criteria, say
someone who:

- Likes you the best?
- Gives you good assignments?
- Never questions you?
- Never pressures you?
- Acknowledges and rewards each accomplishment?

In some ways, the rescue fantasy is a marvelous distraction. While you cling
to your fantasy about how things ought to be at work, you don't work to
relieve your own anxiety and discomfort. You may prefer fantasizing instead
of acknowledging your own role in creating your pain.

Nora Plays the Victim

Nora is the information security consultant from chapter one who's just been
warned about yelling at the client. She firmly believes the universe is out to
get her. The day her car broke down, she blamed the mechanic for not warning her of a potential problem. When she missed the bus to work, it was the
driver's fault for not slowing down. When she arrived late to the morning
meeting, she believed the group had ignored her by starting the meeting without her. When her boss reprimanded her for being late, she felt picked on
because he refused to listen to her explanation about her car. Her horrible
morning kept feeding her evidence that she was suffering.

Nora derives pleasure from playing the victim role; at times she revels
in it. In counseling with me, she described the problems her broken car created in excruciating detail, with dramatic language and a certain comedic flair.
The broken car wasn't just an inconvenience, it was high tragedy. She described how her teammates put their little pointy heads together and con-
spired to make her feel unneeded by starting without her. Her boss was impossible, utterly unreasonable, a demonic force among women. Despite her
laughter, Nora felt hurt, misunderstood, and victimized.

Nora learned her victim role at an early age. She grew up in a home
where tension and crises reigned. Problems with money, violent fights between her alcoholic parents, and older brothers frequently in jail created an
environment of constant chaos. As children of alcoholic parents frequently
do, Nora felt helpless to stop her parents from drinking and fighting. As an
adult, Nora still feels unable to change what upsets her. She doesn't see how
she creates the upsetting situations that evoke her victim feelings.

I think of Nora as a "drama queen." She seems to feel more alive when she's starring in her melodrama. She creates crises and chaos in the workplace to unconsciously recreate the setting she grew up in. As unpleasant as her childhood home was, it's a familiar setting for her. When things happen beyond her control, she chooses to feel personally hurt because unhappiness is familiar to her and harmony is not.

It's Not My Fault!

In your life movie, whether you feature the victim role or just play it occasionally, it's always an attempt to blame others for your problems. It's easier to blame another entity for your misery than to look into yourself for solutions. As the victim, you don't have to blame yourself for the choices you made; playing the victim insulates you from the pain of accountability.

Georgia had difficulty saying *no* and setting limits for herself. She wanted to be seen as a cooperative team player, yet she found herself resentful that her co-workers took liberal advantage of her willingness to accept extra assignments. Her supervisor expected her to stay late or to come in on weekends for urgent deadlines. Georgia was also the event planner for office parties and meetings; she loved being needed so much she had trouble saying *no* whenever she was asked to do something.

When I started coaching Georgia, she was so reluctant to refuse any extra assignments that her way of saying *no* was to get sick. That way she had a "legitimate excuse" to withdraw from responsibilities. Her repressed anger and resentment contributed to health problems. Only when poor health frightened her did Georgia became motivated enough to drop the victim role and learn how to set appropriate boundaries.

It's extremely hard to admit that you think or feel like a victim because of a compelling need for sympathy and attention. In fact, when you are feeling victimized, nothing upsets you faster than to be told you are acting childish. Your defenses are up; deep down you know your behavior is immature, but you're so caught up in your victim role that you don't want to admit it. Yet if you've ever felt it's *you* versus *them* (whomever *them* may be)—you versus some big unidentifiable, undefeatable entity—then you've played the victim role. Of course, you're not alone. We all do this from time to time. When this happens, we need to call on our mental adult director to point out that we're playing the victim role.

If you hang on to outdated beliefs about employer-employee relationships, you are choosing to feel victimized by the company. For instance, you may choose to cling to the belief that a company should take care of its employees as they did in bygone times. Most companies today don't reward loyalty as they used to, but that does not mean that they are victimizing their employees.

Of course, some situations are victimizing. If you are continually passed over for promotions because of your race, culture, gender, or looks, you could consider yourself a victim. However, it's still your choice to feel victimized by this situation. As Eleanor Roosevelt said, "No one can make you feel inferior without your consent."

Viktor Frankl wrote about his experiences as a prisoner in a World War II concentration camp in his book *Man's Search for Meaning*. In a brutal and inhumane situation, Frankl chose not to think of himself as a victim. While he had no control over his captors, he always believed he was in control of his reactions. He believed he either could be a defeated prisoner of war or reframe the situation. He chose to reframe the situation and change his reactions.

Fortunately, most of us do not have to endure such harrowing experiences, but like Frankl, we can choose how to respond to unpleasant situations beyond our control. If you face discrimination because of race, age, weight, gender, or sexual orientation, among other things, your focusing on feeling victimized keeps you stuck in the victim role.

I don't mean to suggest that you should tolerate discrimination or pretend it doesn't exist. I have worked with many people from minority groups, as well as women, gays and lesbians, people with disabilities, and obese people. They are keenly aware of prejudices and biases in the workplace. Yet even when bigotry is present, you can always choose how to react to it. Theresa made a choice not to feel victimized by the racial discrimination she's encountered in her life. She told me, "I choose not to pay attention to racism at work unless it's really blatant. I decided a long time ago that I won't spend my time looking for it. If someone treats me in a negative way or says something racist to me, I see it as *their* problem. If it's really offensive, I first confront them; if that doesn't work, I go through the proper channels. I never stay stuck in negative feelings because it drains my power for everything else."

Ben, on the other hand, chooses to see racism in every problem at work that doesn't go his way. His manager and co-workers describe him as having a chip on his shoulder that severely inhibits his effectiveness on the job. While coaching Ben, I heard stories of a miserable family life, poverty, drug addiction, and abuse. Ben had been a childhood victim of racism and many other personal, family, and educational problems. His past intruded in his present;

Ben saw most of his life through the lens of racism, them versus us, the down-trodden minority. Ben was stuck in hurt, frustration, and anger; he was choosing to blame others for all his difficulties. He was giving away his own personal power by staying stuck in this painful reactive position.

In a research experiment, birds were trained not to go near the closed door of a cage. After the birds were well trained, the door was opened. None of the birds flew out of the cage. They were captives of learned behavior, and they remained captives in their cages. Your belief that you are a victim keeps you captive in emotional bondage more limiting and destructive than anything society perpetuates.

Some people play the victim because they feel powerless. Some have felt so victimized throughout their life that they can't imagine being in charge of writing their own positive scenes or directing their own wonderful life. The fact is, however, they have always been in charge. They have been, and still are, in charge of being a victim.

The victim role is emotional quicksand. You can let yourself sink deeper and deeper until you are engulfed by helpless and powerless feelings. I think most people know at some level, perhaps unconsciously, that they are responsible for their feelings. It can be very difficult to let go of beliefs you've held since childhood, but losing the victim mentality and owning your feelings lead to an emotional prosperity that is intrinsically rewarding.

Playing Victim

1. Look at the responses you wrote down for exercise 1-A in chapter one on pages 13 and 14. Look at the beliefs you have about work and how the workplace should be. Which beliefs reflect victim thinking?

2. Look at your responses for exercise 1-C in chapter one on page 27. Identify scripts where you play the victim role. If you have trouble identifying when you played the victim role, substitute the words *helpless* and *powerless* for *victim* and then see which responses apply.

3. Think about difficult situations at work and how you respond. In which of these situations are you playing the victim role? If it's difficult to identify—or admit—when you're playing the victim role, think about the words you use to describe your situation. "My back is to the wall," "There's nothing I can do," and "I just work here" are all victim statements.

You Are the Director of Your Own Success

The producer of a movie brings together the director, actors, and scriptwriters. As the producer of your own life movie, you bring together the director, actor, and scriptwriter inside of you. You probably are aware only of being the actor in your life movie. Yet you also have the ability to be the director and to detach from the scene and from your feelings to take a careful, objective look at the role you are playing and the script you are using. As the director, you can reframe the scene and look at it differently. You can question the actor: What role are you playing? Is it the role you want to play? Does it work for you or would another role work better to help you get what you want?

The director also studies the script to see if it works. Does it help the actor or is it getting in the way? What needs to be changed? The director then calls on the scriptwriter to make revisions and to create a more successful script that will help the actor be a success.

As we begin to look at your roles and scripts in the next chapters, I often will ask you to take the viewpoint of the director to help you objectively see what you are doing and to examine the current validity and appropriateness of your old scripts. I'll also ask you to have the scriptwriter standing by to rewrite your old scripts so that you, as the actor, can play a role of success.

Stop Making Excuses

Looking at your past helps you understand the scripts you've been using and why you've chosen to cling to scripts that virtually guarantee your misery. Clients often share elaborate explanations of how their mothers hurt them or their fathers ignored them—"This is why I have so many problems today! This is why I suffer so much!"

So what? "Yes," I say, "your childhood was the pits, and your parents didn't give you what you wanted. What are you going to do right now to deal with the problems you face today?"

I'm not indifferent to their pain, but I want them—and you—to understand that a painful childhood is not a good reason to use old scripts that continue to cause suffering today. Do you really want your childhood to define who you are today? Maybe you were helpless then, but you are not helpless as an adult. You have the maturity and sophistication to see what's not working for you, and you have the ability and creativity to write a new script and direct yourself in a new life's movie.

Making Choices

Think about a situation at work that bothers you. Use the questions in the following exercise to explore the options you have and determine what choices you can make.

1. Can you change the situation? Where do you have control?

2. List the specific things you would have to do to change the situation.

3. Are you willing to do these things?
—If yes, when will you do them?
—If no, why not? Are you playing the victim? What are you getting out of playing this role?

4. If you can't change the situation, can you change your reactions?

5. Are you willing to change your reaction?
—If no, why not? Are you playing the victim? Why are you choosing to continue to feel the way you do?

Part Two

Camera!

Reframe and Focus to Revise Your Scripts

Chapter 4

Framing the Big Picture

Do you ever wonder why we love the movies so much? I think it's because movies give us an entertaining and often compelling way to view any aspect of life, fact or fiction. Moviemaking technology provides exciting, inventive ways to shift focus, alter perspective, and see the normally unseeable. Movies can slow time, speed time, go forward, go backward, zoom into microscopic worlds, or zoom out to the cosmos. All these shifting perspectives give us an opportunity to view situations in a different way.

Movies also tell human stories. Movies help us feel things. It's amazing how a series of still pictures printed on celluloid and passed before a projection lamp has the power to make us laugh or cry, shriek or gasp. Movies are a wonderful marriage between technology and human consciousness, and that's why thinking about your life and career through the moviemaking metaphor is so powerful. You have been watching movies most of your life, and if you turn that film-watching experience into consciousness-raising, you can make your scenarios for success become real.

In this chapter, we talk about framing. In moviemaking, framing is how the Director of Photography positions the camera to tell a story by emphasizing certain features of the visual panorama. She or he will use a wide-angle lens, a close-up, or a zooming motion to highlight something for the audience. In consciousness, framing means much the same thing—how you frame something means how you view or perceive an event or situation. To reframe it is to take a different view of it.

How People Frame Their Work

Here is how five different people frame their philosophy about work.

Laurie: I love my job. I have learned and grown so much. My work gives me opportunities to express myself and do productive things. Being productive makes me feel good about myself. I have always had terrific bosses and have worked with many wonderful people over the years. I look forward to going to work, and I adore the challenges in my job.

Wayne: Work is fine. I have some good days, some bad days. I'm doing the best I can, but I know I could do better. If I were more ambitious, I could make more money, but . . . I don't know . . . I guess I'm just not the ambitious type.

Randy: Work's okay. It would be better if I had a more understanding boss who didn't ride me so much.

Joanne: Work is my life. I have a really demanding job, and the company just wants more and more from me. I don't get to spend as much time with my family as I would like because I'm always working. When I stop long enough to think about it, I wonder if it's all worth it.

Ken: I only work because I have to. It isn't wonderful; it's a drag. I have to deal with a bunch of idiots. I work for a jerk—he must have had friends in high places to get promoted. People who say work is great are either lying through their teeth or saying it because they're afraid they might lose their jobs. Work is what you have to do to survive—it's not supposed to be fun and games.

Which of these views about work do you most closely identify with? Perhaps you relate to parts of several views.

Where do these views about work come from? Why is there such a wide range of viewpoint—from the woman who adores her job to the man who despises everything about his job?

Where Our Views Come From

In chapter one I described how your belief system was established. As we grew up, we heard our parents talk about work. From their words and observable behavior, we formed our ideas about work, bosses, and being an employee. All this was going on at the same time we were developing our beliefs about ourselves, other people, and the world at large. Both our joys and our miseries in the workplace relate to those belief systems we formed long ago in childhood.

Let's look now at how your belief system affects what you think and, in turn, what you feel and how you act in today's workplace.

How Our Reactions Are Created

When something happens, you react. The computer freezes while you're saving a file, and you react. Maybe you pout; maybe you scream; maybe you pound the desk; maybe you break out into a cold sweat. Maybe you take it in good humor, or maybe you panic. Your reaction to your crashing computer—or anything else that happens to you—stems from your belief system.

To look more closely at how we form these reactions, I want to introduce you to the work of Albert Ellis, a pioneer in the field of cognitive therapy. Ellis looked at how beliefs affect emotional and mental states and govern behavior. He identified the process we go through in response to an event. His work will help you understand how to rewrite your scripts. You'll see that changing any one of the four elements that Ellis identified—your beliefs, thoughts, feelings, or behavior—leads to changes in the other three elements.

Here is how Ellis described the process you go through in response to events in your life.

- First something happens. This is the *event*. Then you perceive or interpret that event through the filter created by your belief system. This is your perception, or *belief*.
- Next, you have some ideas about your perception of the event. These are your *thoughts*.
- Once your thoughts distill your perception of the event, these thoughts create emotional *feelings*.
- Finally, your feelings lead to actions, or *behavior*.

Let's look at each stage in this process to see what happens and to understand how our beliefs, thoughts, feelings, and actions interrelate. As we do this, I would like you to take the viewpoint of the director as I described in chapter three to maintain objectivity.

Step 1—Your Perception and Belief of an Event Creates Your Thoughts

When something happens, we respond with a thought, an opinion, a judgment, or an evaluation that is determined by our belief system. For example, Wayne, who is manager of the four other staff members introduced above, announces at Thursday's staff meeting that everyone needs to come in on

Saturday to complete a project. Those sitting around the conference table respond in various ways based on their individual belief systems.

Laurie believes that work comes first, and that she should do whatever it takes to get the job done. She thinks, "I'll be there. We have to get this done on time."

Randy believes that family is sacred, and he has plans for his child's softball game on Saturday. He thinks, "This is terrible. My manager has no respect for my personal life."

Ken believes that work should take place only between 8A.M. and, 5P.M. Monday through Friday. He thinks, "You gotta be kidding. I don't do Saturdays."

Joanne believes that managers reward loyalty and recognize people who are willing to go the extra mile. She thinks, "I don't like it, but if you want me there, I'll be there. It'll look good on my evaluation."

Different belief systems give rise to different thoughts. Each person perceived the manager's announcement a little differently based on the filter of his or her belief system.

Misperceptions often create thoughts that lead to unnecessary angst. In another department, Issac talks with Ginger about a presentation he gave the day before. He says, "I think Sally hated my presentation. The whole time she sat in the back of the room with a sour look on her face."

"I heard her tell someone she liked your presentation," Ginger says. "What do you mean she had a sour look?"

Isaac scrunches up his face. "She looked like this."

Ginger chuckles. "Isaac," she says, "Sally's blind as a bat and vain as a high-fashion model. She refuses to wear glasses. She couldn't see your slides from the back of the room. She was squinting!"

Isaac's misinterpretation of Sally's expression lead to a wrong conclusion. To him, Sally's scrunched-up face is a sign of displeasure. Besides that, he has worn glasses most of his life, and he cannot imagine anyone being too vain to wear glasses.

Step 2—Your Thinking Creates Your Feelings

The feelings you have don't come from events; they come from your thinking. Thinking creates your feelings and reactions. If you think that being called Mr. Smith by the secretarial staff is a show of respect, what happens when one of them calls you Carl? Do you feel insulted? Or is she merely being friendly?

It all depends on your belief system and on how you choose to feel. Your preconceptions and expectations create your thoughts and feelings, which in turn guide the choices you make.

Returning to the meeting table, we find that each person has a different feeling because each one had a different thought. Laurie, who thought, "We have to get this done on time," feels determined and loyal. Randy, who believes family is sacred, thinks that work on Saturday invades his personal life. He feels distressed and frustrated. Ken, who thinks work should never extend past five o'clock on Friday, also feels angry, perhaps even outraged. Joanne, who believes in advancing her career by being a team player, feels ambivalent. She doesn't relish giving up her Saturday, but she feels good about pleasing her manager.

Most of us assume that we cannot control our feelings. Many of us believe it is the other way around—that our feelings control us! Our feelings just seem to happen.

In fact, our thoughts trigger our feelings. If an event creates upsetting thoughts, you will have upsetting feelings. If an event creates pleasant thoughts, you will have pleasant feelings. It may be hard to imagine that you could create a new or different feeling, yet the fact is that you—and you alone—are the director of your feelings. You are always in control. It's dangerous to let your feelings run the show. If you do, you're letting the acting-out child take control of your movie. As the adult, you can step in and take charge.

Step 3—Your Feelings Generate Your Actions

Your feelings give rise to your behaviors. If you feel a certain way, you behave accordingly. We could also say that you behave in a way that is consistent with your beliefs, which form the basis of your thoughts and feelings.

Back to the staff members seated around the table, we can imagine behaviors they'll exhibit to express their feelings. Laurie, feeling loyal and determined, may say immediately to Wayne, "You can count on me. I'll be here at 9 A.M. sharp!" Randy, feeling angry and put-upon, may say in a sharp voice, trying to control his anger, "You know, some of us have another life outside of work. I'll try to make it, but I don't know for sure." Ken may say nothing, but will express his feelings of outrage by leaning far back in his chair, crossing his arms over his chest, and fixing his eyes on Wayne, all the time shaking his head back and forth. Joanne, juggling conflicting feelings, may hesitate before finally saying in long, drawn-out syllables, "Well, if we really have to . . . ."

Managers Have Belief Systems, Too

How Wayne, the manager, responds to the reactions of his staff will depend on his belief system. If his belief system holds that employees should not question their managers, he may become even more authoritarian or rigid. If he believes that his staff must like him, he'll be very concerned that everyone feels okay about working on the weekend. He may even try to manipulate employees to get what he wants without making them angry. Pauline, a manager in another department, often asks her staff to stay late or to work on weekends. She uses a sweet-little-girl voice to request extra hours. She drops her head to one side, sighs deeply, and then says, "I hope you won't be mad at me, guys . . . but, I really need your help this weekend . . . you won't let me down, okay?" This technique worked well when, as a child, she would ask her gruff father for something.

Yet another manager, Bert, believes it is important to be liked by his staff. Fearing that his staff will fume if asked to work late, he uses a different manipulative technique. He gathers them together, explains in detail how critical the situation is, and then asks them for their advice. He knows that several people will offer to come in on the weekend and that their offer will nudge the rest of the group to go along with the plan. In this way, Bert never looks like the bad guy because, after all, the bright idea to work the weekend came directly from the staff. These three managers, like their employees, bring their belief systems into the workplace to create complicated scenarios.

Irrational Thinking

We tend to think of ourselves as rational beings, and most of the time we probably are. However, the truth is that our thoughts are not always rational. Our belief system may be faulty or outdated and thus give rise to irrational thoughts. When our thinking doesn't make sense, the feelings and the behaviors that arise may be irrational, too.

"Stinkin' thinkin' " is the phrase that twelve-step programs for addiction use to describe the irrational thinking that comes from a faulty filter. This irrational thinking can sabotage and defeat us. People in twelve-step programs understand that stinkin' thinkin' drives them back to their self-destructive, addictive behaviors.

Here is how it works. A belief that you are your job makes you personalize your job performance evaluations. You will interpret your manager's criticism of your work on a project as a criticism of you as a person. You are using stinkin' thinkin' if making one mistake propels you into feeling like a hopeless failure who will never get it right.

In this thinking, we hear the voice of the internal parent, the voice that attacks our creative thinking, hopes, and desires. The goals, visions, and aspirations we have for ourselves get trashed. The negative voice mocks our desire to change our life for the better. Stinkin' thinkin' perpetrates the powerless feelings we often experienced as children.

You have to explore your belief system to understand why your thinking may be irrational. Remember that your belief system was formed during childhood; the filter through which you interpret events is a childhood invention. If you made a false presumption as a child, you created a faulty filter. It may be that your filters from childhood are no longer applicable to your current situation, and perhaps you haven't updated them yet.

Andy, the research company manager, is paralyzed by his irrational thinking. He believes he cannot afford to make a mistake, so he delays making decisions. He believes the key to making the right decision is to have lots of information, so he keeps sending his employees out to gather more data. Then he criticizes them for the data they provide. The faulty thinking he learned from his parents holds him back from making decisions— not good in a fast-paced industry that prospers on rapid product delivery.

Andy is following a childhood script. As a child, you developed scripts within the family setting as strategies to interact with your parents, siblings, and others to help you get what you wanted. As you developed that script, you didn't ponder other ways to think or feel or behave; a child doesn't have the sophistication to evaluate options. You created one way, and it seemed to work, so you used it again and again. Now you're no longer a child, but you may be continuing to use the same strategies with a different cast of players. You may think the same thoughts, have the same feelings, and react in the same way you did as a child. You may be reacting to people and challenges at work the same way you reacted as a five-year-old or ten-year-old child.

You continue to re-enact these old scripts repeatedly so that they become automatic. What does automatic mean? It means that you can do something without thinking about it; that your reaction is involuntary. But it also means that as soon as you stop thinking about it, you stop being aware of your options, and then you can't make choices.

The Critic

We often hold an internal dialogue with ourselves that some call "self-talk." I think of it as the critic, which is an expression of our private thoughts about ourselves and the world. The voice of the critic can be good if the dialogue is positive and loving. ("Thumbs way up!") However, more frequently the critic is hostile and self-destructive, and we hear the voice of the harsh critic. ("Thumbs way down! What was I thinking when I made that pathetic excuse of a movie!")

Negative beliefs such as "I'm a terrible person," "Something is wrong with me," and "I'm not good enough" become the jumping-off points for a swarm of rambling, irrational, negative thoughts. It's as if you took the thought and stretched it to its most irrational extreme. Someone's complaint about something you did evokes the thought, "I messed up on this again," quickly followed by "It figures; I'm an idiot. I can't do anything right." When this happens, you're letting the cruel voice of the critic tear you down and defeat you. In the cesspool of sheer misery, it's hard to remember that this monster is mostly the result of automatic thinking.

Penelope grew up in a family of brilliant but critical parents and overachieving, successful older brothers. She often felt that no matter how hard she worked, no matter what she did, her efforts weren't enough. Penelope could never live up to her family's expectations. She felt she wasn't smart enough, popular enough, or pretty enough. In shame, she'd retreat to her bedroom and cry. She brought these feelings of inadequacy to the workplace in a publications group, a highly stressful environment of deadlines and last-minute changes. When the demands and pressures got to her and she felt overwhelmed, the feelings of inadequacy from childhood came flooding back. Penelope became emotionally paralyzed, and she burst into tears, gripped by the old belief: I am not good enough. She had to work hard with me to replace this faulty premise with a positive belief: I am capable; I work hard; I produce excellent results.

Short Circuiting

We normally don't separate our thoughts from our feelings, or even realize that our thoughts are the source of our feelings. Usually, we're just aware that something happens, we feel a certain way, and then we act.

Imagine that a co-worker in a staff meeting questions the project plan you presented last week. You interrupt and say angrily, "Look, Diane, we've gone over this several times already, and last week everyone agreed with the dates and action items. If you had a problem with it, you should have brought it up then." You're not aware of the thoughts that created the feelings of anger.

What you're probably aware of is that you feel angry. It may be that every time you feel angry, you think you have to attack or fend off the person who upset you. You're reacting without conscious thought instead of acting with conscious intention.

This is like that example of being poked in an elevator. Someone pokes you, and you instantly (it seems) get annoyed. The next poke instantly (so it seems) escalates the feeling to anger. If you let the feeling run you and don't think any more about it, you might whirl around in a rage and glare at, yell at, or even punch whomever poked you.

If that example seems extreme, here's a common workplace situation: the copier is jammed again. What do you do? Do you immediately feel frustrated and jab the start button repeatedly as if it'll magically heal itself? Do you instantly get angry and growl at the first administrative assistant you see, "When are you going to fix this damn thing?" You believe that the expensive copier is supposed to work perfectly when you need it. A nonworking copier ignites your anger.

In emotional situations, feelings arise so quickly that you don't even realize you went through the steps of perceiving the event, interpreting the event, and then having thoughts about it. Instead, like a short circuit, you go from event to feelings to action. It happens so rapidly that you don't remember you had a choice about what your feeling could be, and even earlier, what your thoughts could be. You don't realize you had options, and that you made choices. When you replay your response process in mental slow-motion, however, you get a fascinating view of how your emotions erupt and where you could insert new choices on how to feel.

Another short-circuiting scenario happens when you experience unpleasant feelings and you instantly block the feelings from your awareness. You go directly from the event (the stimulus) to your behavior (the response). When your response isn't pretty, you may end up apologizing for your behavior, saying something like, "Gee, I'm sorry I said that. I don't know why I said it."

Yes, you *do* know why! The healthy place inside you where your director resides knows what's going on and why you say or do things. Explaining why you reacted as you did may bring up unpleasant and closely-guarded memories from the past. The feelings remind you of when you felt powerless as a child. It's easier to apologize than to face the old painful feelings.

Concealing Feelings

You can develop some elaborate strategies to avoid owning your feelings, particularly uncomfortable feelings. Nobody likes feeling jealous or angry or humiliated or afraid. These are not easy emotions to handle. You may find these feelings so uncomfortable that when something occurs to bring them up, you launch into a concealing act.

You learned very early as a child that it's not a good idea to express certain feelings. For example, an older sibling may have taunted and teased you, and when you showed that you were hurt, you got a more vicious taunting. So you hid your feelings by making a sarcastic comment. Or perhaps you let the hurt feeling fester, later expressing your pain with a hostile comment that shot out of the blue.

Since you perceived it was dangerous to express how you really felt, you developed masking behaviors. Sometimes you become so good at concealment that you also hide your real feelings from yourself. The original feeling is still there, but it's been repressed and subverted into something else.

Some people use sarcasm, put-downs, or belittling remarks to conceal feelings such as envy, disappointment, anger, or fear. Remember the fable of the fox who tried to reach a bunch of grapes hanging overhead? When his attempts failed, he grumbled, "Those grapes were sour anyway." When people try for something and they don't get it, they sometimes belittle the desired object with a sour-grapes attitude. "I didn't really want to win that trophy anyway," they say, trying to conceal their keen disappointment.

When a co-worker is promoted, you may hear people say things like, "Yeah, well, we all know who the teacher's pet is." Remarks like these are cover-ups for the speaker's envy or resentment. When Vanessa heard about Lenore's promotion, she put Lenore down by calling her an apple-polisher. She told herself that the promotion and VP title were not a big deal; that anybody could get one.

Envy is not an easy emotion to cope with. Most of us don't like admitting to being jealous over someone else's success. This powerful emotion may unconsciously remind you of childhood when you were rivals with your siblings for your parents' attention. As a child, Vanessa was told by her mother,

"Now don't you be jealous of your little sister. She's getting the extra toy because she's younger." The message Vanessa took to heart was that jealousy should not be expressed directly. She developed a coping strategy and wrote a script similar to that of the fox and the sour grapes.

Lenore's promotion also triggered abandonment feelings for Vanessa. When the two worked together as analysts, they related as peers. That peer relationship ended when Lenore took the supervisor's job and returned to school to advance her career. Vanessa realized upon reflection that she felt Lenore had abandoned her when she opted to leave the analyst position for the supervisory position. The same thing happened when her best friend in childhood broke off their friendship to start playing with other girls at school. Back then, Vanessa dealt with her feelings by calling her best friend names and acting as if she didn't care that she'd been left behind. She relied on that same old jealousy script to cope with her feelings about Lenore.

When your feelings are deeply uncomfortable, you may repress or deny them to avoid the discomfort. As uncomfortable as some feelings can be, you will be better off—more in charge of writing a winning script—if you don't ignore those feelings.

Acknowledging them doesn't mean you have to act on them. It simply means you recognize that they exist. Uncomfortable feelings give us clues and cues about our hidden desires. When you insult someone with a belittling remark, you most likely long for something the other person has—wealth, prestige, beauty, power, superiority. You may not want the whole package of who they are, but you probably want a piece of it. For example, you may envy the attention your manager lavishes on a co-worker because you want to be recognized by your manager, too.

If you don't acknowledge your true feelings, they will most likely stay with you, and you will eventually express them in ways that can harm you. Sarcastic digs may initially amuse your peers, but you could gain a reputation for being cruel, too. Then people may become less trusting of you because they don't want your caustic spray directed at them. They may find it is safer simply to keep their distance.

Your feelings can also bloat and mutate into something uglier. Until Vanessa accepted her envy of Lenore's success and her feelings of being abandoned, she could barely speak to Lenore. Her feelings threatened to poison their relationship and to embitter Vanessa so that the toxins could have spread into relationships with other co-workers.

Acknowledging unpleasant feelings does not mean you have to share your feelings with others. It just means that you become aware of them and stay honest with yourself about what you're feeling. Think of these awkward and uncomfortable feelings as an inner voice that can point out your needs and desires. It's a voice that can help you understand better where your vulnerable spots are. Like director's notes in a movie script, it informs the actor of internal motivation.

Change for the Better

You can change your thoughts, feelings, and behaviors, which means you can change your script. The first step toward making any change is to understand what's going on. Start by looking at your belief system because that's what underpins it all.

To do this, peer back into your history and look at how your script was developed. If you don't understand your past, you are doomed to repeat it. Most of us have been repeating the past through our scripts because we never had the tools to realize how we wrote our scripts in the first place. Looking at how you developed your coping strategies as a child will help you rewrite your script so that it is appropriate at work. Meanwhile, looking back at childhood experiences as an adult director may lead you to some very different conclusions.

Separate Yourself From Your Script

You are not your beliefs. You are not your thoughts, your feelings, or your behaviors. You need to separate "you" the "actor" from the script you're enacting.

We go to the workplace with our old ghostwritten scripts, our heads filled with beliefs and emotions from the past. Even though many of our old childhood defense and coping mechanisms don't apply in our present circumstances, we still activate them.

Type-cast actors always play the same type of role in every film they make. They are renowned for their predictability. Good actors are flexible; they adapt and change, and they use different techniques that are appropriate for the different plots they are in and the different roles they play.

Are You Being Realistic?

You have to be realistic about whether or not all your needs can be met in the workplace. Some needs just cannot be fulfilled at work. Harlan unconsciously wanted to recreate the closeness he had enjoyed as a child in a large family, which he now missed. He looked to his co-workers to satisfy this need and tried to create a family in the workplace. Every Monday morning he would ritualistically visit each person's cubicle to chat about everyone's weekend. He fussed over people's birthdays, paying for cakes and cards out of his own pocket. He brought in doughnuts for the staff meetings. He never went to lunch alone, but always invited someone in the office to join him.

Yet the family setting Harlan sought to duplicate in the workplace never materialized to his expectations. He was disappointed when several co-workers went to lunch and did not ask him to join them. He grew angry that no one volunteered to share the expense of the doughnuts and birthday offerings. He was deeply hurt when he noticed people stepping away from their cubicles as he approached. He felt devastated and betrayed when he heard that most of the staff had gotten together for drinks one night after work, and no one had invited him.

Although Harlan's need for a family-like closeness with his co-workers was strong, it was unrealistic, especially in a workplace where people valued their independence. His neediness drove people away. His need could not be satisfied in most American workplaces. Most people separate their families from their work. Harlan needed to look for the closeness he sought by developing friends outside of work.

Your boss is not your parent. It's unrealistic to expect your boss to protect you, nurture you, or make you feel good about yourself. Similarly, your co-workers are not your siblings. It's unrealistic to expect them to be your best pals, to listen to your problems, or to remember your birthday. You can't keep bringing your needy internal child into the workplace. One manager, Samantha, told me recently that she'd given up babysitting as an adolescent and won't do that now for her employees. Harlan would not get sympathy from Samantha, but would elicit impatience and disgust.

Family Businesses

It can be very difficult to separate personal issues from appropriate workplace behavior in family-owned businesses. I have mediated numerous conflict-resolution sessions among family members whose effectiveness and communications break down when parents are bosses and siblings are co-workers. All the family history is present every day at work as they continue to replay old feelings, roles, and behavior patterns with bosses and co-workers who are also their relatives.

Old scenarios of sibling rivalry, competing for parents' attention, manipulation, and frequent temper tantrums are typical in a family-owned business. The successful members are able to stay adult, with clearly defined roles and responsibilities, specific succession plans, concrete benefits, and promotion plans.

Louie, now seventy years old, inherited several family-owned dry goods stores from his father, who died about fifteen years ago. Louie and his wife, Alma, who also worked in the stores throughout her career, encouraged their three children, Lou Jr., Steve, and Vicki, to learn the retail business. The children worked after school, on weekends, and during summers. Louie is now CEO and president. Lou Jr. is chief operating officer; Steve is vice president of marketing and sales; and Vicki is chief financial officer. Although Louie and Alma go on cruises, play golf, and are socially active in their country club, their presence is always felt as owners of the business.

Louie truly controls decisions that Lou Jr. makes about the business and then sabotages them. Alma is still involved, laying frequent guilt trips on her children when they don't perform to her expectations. Steve resents his older brother's position, and Lou Jr. thinks Steve's plans to expand are grandiose and extravagant. As CFO, Vicki often sides with Lou Jr. and vetoes Steve's marketing ideas. Employees are confused about from whom to take orders. They often hear Lou Jr., Steve, and Vicki arguing behind closed doors. Vicki resents making less money than her brothers, especially since she holds such a responsible position. Her parents remind her that her husband makes enough to support her.

By the time I was called in, a crisis was in full swing. In tears, Vicki had quit her job during month-end financial reports. She refused to talk to any family member and just wanted to be bought out. It took many months of working with the entire family as a group and as individuals to help them separate their professional responsibilities from their family roles and communication patterns. Steve ended up selling his share to the rest of the family when he realized his business philosophies and marketing approaches were incompatible with theirs. Vicki trained a controller so she could spend more time with her own family and went part-time. My greatest victory was getting them to commit to an agreement that business would not be discussed at family get-togethers. I continue to work with this family when they need a neutral party to facilitate their meetings and keep them on track in a professional way.

Analyzing Feelings

Tony is a sales rep with a hidden belief problem—he thinks there's something bad about making tons of money as a top salesman. While he has a knack for selling, he occasionally jeopardizes a sale through forgetfulness. One time he forgot to get key signatures on a contract. Another time he forgot an appointment with an important client. He blamed these glitches on drinking too much when things got stressful. Tony had not yet realized that the stress arose whenever he was on the verge of making the big sale that would hoist him over his sales goals and make him the top salesperson in his territory.

Tony's actions today can be traced back to the beliefs he developed as a child. His father never finished high school and struggled for years to earn a living in different blue collar jobs—construction worker, janitor, security guard. He often complained about management's lack of respect for the workers. "They think they're better than we are," he'd grumble. A football star in high school, his father frequently expressed frustration that he'd never been able to play pro football, forced instead to work in low-paying jobs. In response, Tony's deeply religious mother would reassure his father that money and status were not important in God's eyes. Money and material wealth kept people from being "kind and loving to their fellow man," she was fond of saying.

His parents seemed unimpressed when Tony's good grades won him a college scholarship. He thought he might have pleased them more had he been more athletic like his father or more religious like his mother. In college he discovered he had a natural flair for sales and quickly found a sales position after graduation. Despite his pride at being named Junior Salesman of the Year his first year on the job, he didn't tell his parents. The more successful he became, the more anxiety he felt. Unconsciously, Tony believed that his father would be humiliated if his son surpassed him professionally; he believed his mother would be wounded if she knew how much money he made. Tony was unaware of these thoughts; he only knew that his anxiety soared each time he neared his quarterly goals. After a couple of stiff drinks, he didn't feel as anxious, and the odd little nagging voice in his head whispering "Money is evil" went away.

Tony recently presented a proposal for a health and disability insurance plan to Reuben, the benefits manager of a large corporation. Hoping eventually to get his business, Tony has been talking to Reuben off and on for two years. He was thrilled when Reuben invited him to present his proposal to the company's board of directors. Normally great at making presentations like this, Tony was surprised when the thought of this presentation caused him to sweat and hyperventilate.

Uncomfortable feelings such as anger, frustration, or disappointment can indicate that things are not going as you would like. If you suppress or ignore such feelings, you, like Tony, may experience discomfort in your body. For example, dealing with a difficult person or situation might create tension in your body, leading to a headache, backache, upset stomach, or clenched jaw. Analyzing and dealing with your feelings can make you feel better both physically as well as emotionally.

Tony put on his director's cap and analyzed his situation. The dialogue between Tony and his internal director went like this.

Director: What is the uncomfortable feeling or body discomfort?

Tony: Anxiety, hyperventilating, sweating, knots in my stomach.

Director: On a scale of one to ten, how uncomfortable are you? (A rating of one means you are completely comfortable; a rating of ten means you are extremely uncomfortable.)

Tony: Extremely uncomfortable—ten.

Director: What scene triggers these feelings or discomfort?

Tony: Getting ready to make an important presentation to a client we've been wanting for some time. If I can close this sale, I'll exceed my sales goals for the year and put myself in a good position to be named salesman of the year.

Director: What are the negative beliefs and thoughts you have about yourself or others in this scene?

Tony: If I pull off this sale and then get named salesperson of the year, I'll get a bonus. That's a lot more money than I need to live on comfortably. Do I really need this much money? At the same time, I feel angry that the directors have all this power to make or break the sale based on how my presentation goes. I imagine the directors looking at me and thinking, "Who is this guy?" Well, who the hell are they, anyway? I feel like they're making me jump through hoops to get this sale.

Director: What do you do when you have these feelings and thoughts?

Tony: I have a drink when I'm feeling really anxious.

Director: What did others do that contributed to your feelings and thoughts and behaviors?

Tony: My manager reminded me the other day that this sale is a "biggie" because we've been courting the client for two years. That made me feel even more anxious. I started hyperventilating when he said that.

Director: What is your part in this scene? What are you doing to contribute to it?

Tony: I'm letting myself get anxious. I'm letting negative thoughts and bad feelings take over instead of being focused on what I need to do to prepare for this presentation.

Director: What external things are beyond your control?

Tony: I can't force the client to buy. I can try to influence their decision, but I can't make their decision.

Director: What unrealistic expectations do you hold about how external things should be or should provide for you?

Tony: I'm angry at Reuben for making me give this presentation before the board of directors. But it's unrealistic to expect them to approve this proposal without meeting me and hearing from me. Naturally, they need to be sure that they are making a good decision because this is a big financial commitment.

Director: What internal things do you have control over?

Tony: I can stop paying attention to the negative thoughts and focus instead on imagining success. I can avoid taking that first drink when I start to feel anxious. I can meet with my boss to review my strategy and practice my presentation.

Director: Are the feelings, thoughts, and behaviors connected with this scene familiar to you?

Tony: It seems like I go through something similar every time I have the chance to make a big sale.

Director: Have you experienced similar scenes in other places, such as in other jobs or with other people?

Tony: Yes. Every time I have a chance to make a sale that will earn me a bonus or will put me over the top on my sales goals.

Director: How intense is the feeling or discomfort now?

Tony: It's down to five.

Feelings of Discomfort

Take a few minutes to think about what is going on right now in the theater of your workplace that creates discomfort for you. A difficult person or situation might evoke feelings of anger, frustration, disappointment, sadness, hurt, intimidation, or helplessness.

If you are not aware of uncomfortable or unpleasant feelings, you may be aware of discomfort in your body. This could include tension in some part of your body, such as headache, backache, stiff neck, clenched jaw, upset stomach, or facial tics. Other signs of discomfort may be dry mouth, shortness of breath, or feeling flushed.

The discomfort may come from a particular event, or it may be an ongoing situation. One way to get yourself thinking about this is to ask, "What do I wish I could change at work?"

Take the event or situation you want to change and go through the following series of questions. Since this event will be the basis of other exercises, I suggest you write down your responses for later reference.

Let's also invoke our movie-making metaphor again. Put on your director's cap so you can analyze each scene and examine the roles you are playing and the scripts you are using.

- What is the uncomfortable feeling or body discomfort?
- On a scale of 1 to 10, how intense is the feeling or discomfort?
  (A rating of 1 means it is not intense; 10 means it is extremely intense.)
- What is the situation that triggers these feelings or discomfort?
- What are the negative beliefs and thoughts you have about yourself or others in this scene?

- What do you do when you have these feelings and thoughts?
- What did others do that contributed to your feelings, thoughts, and behaviors?
- What is your part in this scene? What are you doing to contribute to it?
- What external things are beyond your control?
- What unrealistic expectations do you hold about how external things should be or should provide for you?
- What internal things are within your control?
- Are the feelings, thoughts, and behaviors connected with this scene familiar to you?

Pointers to the Past

The one to ten rating Tony gave to his feeling measured the intensity of the feeling. Exercise 4-A asked you to assign a one to ten rating to your feeling. Intense feelings (those with ratings of six or higher) are signs that something from your past should be addressed. You haven't dealt with whatever happened in your past that has created the intensity of today's feeling. When you over react to a situation, your past is interfering with your present.

For example, if you blow up every time someone at work takes a pen or something else from your desk without asking your permission, you are over reacting. No doubt you know this; but why are you over reacting? Perhaps as a child your siblings were constantly taking your things without asking. You were hurt and angry they didn't respect your property back then. You are overly sensitive today to someone borrowing your things because you haven't dealt with the reactions you had as a child.

Flashbacks to Childhood

Flashbacks in the movies are scenes from the past to help you understand what motivates a character today. Flashing back to your own past helps you understand your current motives and why you react today the way you do. That's because these flashbacks identify the sources of your scripts.

Perhaps as an adult you've experienced having your mother talk to you as if you were six years old again. It could be the words she uses, her tone of voice, her facial expression, or her gestures. No doubt your mother is using her mother's script to talk to you, and her script may unconsciously prompt you to pull out your child's script. In that script, when your mother speaks to you a certain way, you may feel powerless, perhaps even disobedient. You may respond just the way you did when you were a child: sullen, silent, and thinking to yourself, "There she goes again!"

Many of my clients get into situations like this with their mothers and are aware of what triggered the flashback. "My mother makes me feel like a child," they say. Of course, they really mean that they're choosing to re-enact their child's script, and that means perpetuating the thoughts, feelings, and behaviors of childhood.

When you are dealing with the cast at work, you probably aren't aware of what triggers your old scripts. You might see a similarity between the way your boss looks when displeased and how your parent looked, and then react the same way you did when you felt like a naughty child. Or the way a co-worker whines about something might remind you of how your younger sister whined. It's no surprise you either ridicule or criticize your co-worker, just as you did your sister.

But often the triggers are much more subtle. You don't realize how something that happens today, or something that someone says to you today, sends you flashing back to the past, but subtle triggers may still be very powerful. Connecting the thoughts and feelings you have today with experiences from your past can help you see when, where, and how your old scripts were written. You can also look at ways to detach from the past so that you can put aside your old scripts and write new ones—that is, to fast forward to the future!

Exercise 4-B will help you launch a flashback to your early experiences and discover the source of your scripts.

When Tony entered a flashback, he explored the anxious feelings he had about being a successful salesperson. He thought back to his childhood and remembered a time he felt the same way as he did now. He was eight years old and had just been given the lead in his class play. At supper that night, he proudly told his parents about his role in the play, and he asked them to come see him when the class performed the following week. His father snorted and said, "My son, the little star, huh? Well, I can't take off work to come see you in some silly school play, Tony. I'd be fired if I did that." His mother said the play fell on the same day she'd volunteered at church to make quilts for needy families. "Couldn't you go to the church on another day?" Tony asked.

"I'm surprised to hear you suggest that," his mother admonished. "You're only thinking of yourself. Other people in this world need our help."

Tony's excitement evaporated, and he thought, "They don't care about me. They don't think my play is very important."

As Tony recalled this episode and worked through the series of questions posed in exercise 4-B, he rated the intensity of his feeling at the time as a nine because his disappointment was strong. The worst thing he believed about himself was, "I'm not okay. I'm selfish because I think my play is so important." The worst thing he believed about his parents was that they didn't love him or care about his achievements. He was angry that his father thought work was more important than his play. Although he really wanted his parents to be proud about his role in the play and to watch him perform, he dropped the issue, fearing he'd be rebuffed again.

Tony realized that the life script he developed from this experience was that his achievements didn't matter and he shouldn't be proud of them. He learned to minimize his accomplishments. When he thought about his job in sales, he began to understand why he sabotaged his chances for success and glory as an adult. He linked success with being selfish. If that success included money and recognition, such as a hefty bonus for being salesman of the month, he'd think of his mother's speech about needy people and feel guilty.

Flashbacks

For this exercise, find a place to relax and let yourself get into a quiet frame of mind. Take a few deep breaths to let go of any tension before you begin. Some people find that closing their eyes helps them flash back to earlier experiences.

Use the situation you worked on in exercise 4-A on page 94. Remember the feelings and thoughts you experienced in this workplace scene. As you focus on the scene, attempt to link it to your child self— when in your childhood do you remember feeling or thinking the same way? Try to recall the earliest time you can remember experiencing these same feelings and thoughts.

Some people have trouble remembering their childhood experiences. If you can't recall your childhood, start by recalling a more recent time when you experienced these same feelings and thoughts—maybe at a previous job. Recall when you had these same feelings and thoughts in that job. Then go back to the job before that, and recall a time you had these feeling and thoughts. Think about your first job . . . then college . . . high school . . . grade school . . . after-school activities, such as sports or clubs. Trace the feelings and thoughts as far back as possible.

Now take some time to ask yourself the following questions:

1. Recall the details of your earliest flashback experience and record them in your notebook.

- How old were you?
- Was there anyone else in the scene? Who?
- What happened exactly?
- What did you do or say in this flashback scene?
- What did the others in the scene do and say?

- How did you feel?
- On a scale of 1 to 10, how strong was the feeling? (A rating of 1 means "hardly feel" and 10 means "very strong.")
- What were your thoughts?
- What was the very worst thing you believed about yourself? Who told you this thing about yourself? If you can't recall being told this thing directly, who made you believe it?
- What was the worst thing you believed about others in the flashback scene?

2. What did you really want to happen in the flashback scene?
   - What did you do to make it happen?
   - Did that work? Did you get what you wanted?
   - How did it leave you feeling?

3. What was the script you developed to help you cope with or make sense of what happened in the scene from your early experience?

4. Compare your flashback to the workplace situation in exercise 4-A.
   - Are the beliefs, thoughts, feelings, and actions the same or similar in both your flashback and your workplace scene?
   - What other parallels do you see between your flashback and your workplace scene?

Looking at several experiences this way can help you see the pattern of your scripts. Go through the same series of questions for other flashback experiences you recall.

Basic Self-Defeating Beliefs

The flashback analysis process helps you uncover self-defeating beliefs you developed about yourself and are probably not conscious of anymore. These core beliefs are at the root of the feelings you experience at work.

Here are some examples of self-defeating core beliefs that people hold about themselves, representing the worst they believe about themselves.

- I'm not okay.
- I'm a bad person.
- I'm dumb; I'm not smart enough.
- I'm not likable; I'm not lovable.
- Something is wrong with me.
- I'm not good enough.

Which of these negative beliefs do you hold about yourself? What other negative things do you believe about yourself?

When something bad happens that makes us feel miserable, the voice of the critic fills our heads, chanting all the old negative beliefs and repeating the negative judgments we have about ourselves. The negative beliefs create negative thoughts, which stir up negative feelings. While negative beliefs were formed during childhood, they still have crippling, gripping power. They carry such intensity it is difficult to separate past from present. Whatever you thought you were back then, you still think you are now. Analyzing flashbacks from the past helps you see how and when negative beliefs were formed, creating an opportunity to rewrite the script and decrease your anguish.

Detach From the Scene

Emotions from the past can feel as intense now as they did when you first experienced them. You can still get swept up in them during flashbacks. In creating scenarios for your success, you recall childhood experiences to understand your history by exploring the origin of your scripts. I don't want you to wallow in pain from the past. Instead, I want you to use our moviemaking metaphor to guide you through your flashback experience.

Children think the universe revolves around them. Their perspective on the world, metaphorically, is up-close and personal. It's like the tight, in-your-face shots in the movies. That's why you remember scenes from your childhood with such vivid intensity—assuming you let yourself remember them in the first place. In working with scenes from your childhood as an adult, you want to learn to distance and detach yourself from the flashback by taking a wide-angle, big picture, objective view of your experiences. The director of a movie chooses from multiple camera lenses and camera angles to shoot the picture. Scenes can be shot in wide-angle or telephoto, close-up or distant, soft focus or crisp focus, filtered or unfiltered.

The lens the director chooses helps create the emotional effect of the scene in the film. Using this analogy, we often view our lives through a close-up lens created by our emotions. That's what creates the intensity in our recollection of past experiences. The more tightly focused we are on the flashback, the more intense the emotion. We need to pull back to take a longer, wider view. This dilutes the emotions so that we can then examine our past with more objectivity and maturity.

You can use two techniques to create that objectivity. One involves using the camera; the other involves using the director.

Look Through the Camera Lens

To give yourself distance from the childhood scene, replay it while looking through a different camera lens. The camera is objective; it doesn't have an emotion. We'll use a wide-angle camera lens to give you a new way to look at the situation. The wide-angle lens pulls you out of the scene so you can observe the other actors, details, and interactions you probably didn't notice before. You'll see the entire context of the scene. The fresh perspective will be more objective than the close-up lens created by your child-star emotions.

Imagine You Are the Director

The other way to detach is to imagine you are the director watching the rushes from a day's shooting. This director's perspective pulls you out of the child's mind and pops you into the mature adult mind. You'll look rationally and objectively at the scene to see what works for you and what doesn't. Then with the director's help, you'll replace the parts that don't work with new parts that do.

Usually you recall a memory the way you saw it happen—through your eyes from the point of view of where you were at the time. It's as if the camera is right behind your eyes. For example, think about a birthday party when you blew out the candles on the cake. Most likely, as you recall the scene, you see someone, perhaps your mother, holding up the glowing cake and walking toward you. Now the cake is in front of you. You look down to see the bright candles and your name written in frosting. Your family and friends are gathered around the scene, and you look at them smiling and urging you to blow. You take a deep breath, lean forward, and feel the candles' warmth. When you blow hard, you see the flames moving away in trails of smoke, and then you hear a burst of applause and hurrahs.

When you recall things this way, the scene unfolds all around you. You were literally in the middle of the scene when it happened, and now, many years later, you're still in the middle. This is where thoughts and feelings are most intense; the feelings you had then rush back now with the visual memory. It's often hard to separate from the emotions you experienced at the time, but the opportunity to grow is worth the effort.

To give yourself distance to detach from the emotions, recall that birthday party in another way. Rather than being center stage, put yourself outside the scene. Imagine you are videotaping a scene of a child blowing out candles, or you are sitting in a director's chair watching the scene. What do you see now? Several people are gathered around a table in a darkened room. A woman enters the room from the kitchen; she's holding a cake with several lit candles on top. She walks across the room and puts the cake down in front of a child. The other people around the table sing "Happy Birthday," then cry, "Make a wish! Blow out the candles!" The child takes a deep breath, and, with cheeks puffed out, leans over the cake and blows out the candles.

The scene is different. You see it more objectively. You more clearly see the other people in the scene and what's going on for them. Perhaps you see that your father looks tired from a long day's work, and he can't suppress a yawn. Perhaps you see your mother putting down the cake, then turning her attention to the baby, who's starting to cry and fidget in his high chair. Perhaps your older sibling is poking a finger into the frosting.

The scene takes on a completely different perspective. Without the intense emotional coloring of the close-up view, you can look at the bigger picture and come up with a different interpretation. When you pull yourself from center stage where only your needs and emotions fill the screen, you can recognize the other dynamics. Perhaps you're willing to give up your pain that your mother bought a cake with white frosting, not your favorite chocolate. You can see from the director's perspective that she had her hands full with three kids and an exhausted husband. Maybe you can re-evaluate that long-harbored belief that she didn't care what she gave you.

Review the View

Apply the distancing technique to a current situation. In re-examining the situation for this exercise, remain in the adult director role, looking at the event through the objective lens of the camera.

Use the workplace situation you analyzed in exercise 4-A. Replay the scene to see it happening again. As you replay it, distance and detach by imagining you are looking through a camera lens or that you are the director sitting on the sidelines watching the screen unfold. As you watch the scene through the director's eyes, answer these questions:

- Who are the other actors in the scene? What did they say and do? What did you say and do?
- As director, do you see what needs to be different to make the scene more comfortable for you?
- On a scale of 1 to 10, rate how intense the feeling or discomfort is. (A rating of 1 means it is not intense; 10 means it is extremely intense.)
- Compare this rating to your original rating when you recalled this scene in exercise 4-A. Has the number gone down?

Most people find that the rating of their negative feelings in the scene has gone down after they do this exercise. If your rating has not gone down, review the scene gain, this time through an even wider angle lens. Distance yourself and detach. Push back your director's chair and take a very long look at the scene from the sidelines.

The Script Begins to Change

You can see how changing your perception of a scene has an impact on your thoughts and feelings. You can change your perspective through mental techniques similar to how movie-making technology gives directors different ways to change perspective on film and see how that changes your thoughts and feelings.

In the next chapter, we'll explore more specifically how you can challenge and change your beliefs, thoughts, and feelings. Again we will call on the internal director of *My Successful Career.*

Chapter 5

The Director's Challenge
Viewing the Action
Behind the Camera Lens

The Oscar-winning film *Good Will Hunting* is the story of a young math genius who was emotionally crippled by a childhood filled with horrible scenes of abuse. His childhood scripts had a devastating impact on his relationships and career. He could out-think brilliant Ivy League math professors, but he was so paralyzed by his past that he kept a job as a janitor and lived in a ratty old rented room. It wasn't until a psychologist intervened that the young man, Will Hunting, finally broke through his emotional straightjacket.

Change isn't easy and we often resist it. Will Hunting kicked, screamed, and fought change. Yet sometimes we reach a point where we are so desperately miserable that something new needs to happen. We must do something different because the old way doesn't work anymore.

Sometimes it's hard to admit that you need to change. Many people wear their habits like dreary, faded wallpaper, day in and day out. I liken this to a person trying to walk out of a room with his eyes closed. He keeps crashing into the wall, not perceiving that the door is two feet to the left. If you watched this scene as a moviegoer, you'd wonder, "Why is this klutz banging his head against the wall? Why doesn't he open his eyes so he can see where the door is?"

The difficulty that character has in opening his eyes is seeded in a childhood resistance to change. That resistance applies to all sorts of situations where change would be a good idea. If your parents took the path of least resistance, you probably adopted that style of thinking, feeling, and behaving. Much of life's pain happens when life doesn't match your expectations. Consciously or unconsciously, you think, "This isn't how it's supposed to be." The more tightly you cling to your belief of how life is supposed to be, the more discomfort and pain you experience when beliefs collide with reality.

More is at stake today in the workplace if you refuse to change. Your income, career path, reputation, and even your job itself are jeopardized if you resist changing and doggedly insist upon re-enacting your old, outdated scripts. In the movie of your life, *My Successful Career*, you need to look at whether your scripts further the plot and produce the results you want, or whether they keep you repeating the same awkward scenes with the same disappointing results.

We often maintain a childish insistence that others, not us, should change so we can get what we want. Maybe this worked when you were a child, when throwing a tantrum or sulking may have convinced your parents to ease up and back down. The workplace usually won't indulge you the way your parents did, however.

Nora, the information security consultant, is on warning for blowing up at a client. It's not the first time she's been warned. As a child, Nora learned to express her anger by screaming and throwing tantrums in a desperate attempt to get her mother's attention. She's carried this behavior into the workplace, where she deals with her negative feelings by creating unpleasant scenes. When someone disagrees with her, she thinks they don't respect her, and she gets upset and lashes out at them. If someone doesn't follow her advice, she becomes angry because she feels she's being ignored. She threatens or insults them.

Like many children of alcoholics, Nora grew up believing she was to blame whenever anything bad happened. Even when the situation was beyond her control, as when her brother landed in jail or the landlord threatened to evict the family, Nora felt it was her fault it happened. That script persists in her adult life. If something goes wrong because a client failed to follow her recommendation, she still feels personally responsible.

Nora lets herself be controlled by her unhappy inner child, who is starved for attention. She wants people to like and respect her, but her tantrums and verbal attacks repel them. Her blind adherence to her childhood script causes her continuous pain.

Who's Running Your Show?

You can't keep playing the child's role and expect to get what you want. Even child stars grow up. Today's workplace demands we play adult roles; we must rewrite childhood scripts into something appropriate for adults.

Who runs your show? Who's really in charge of *My Successful Career?* The playfulness and creativity of the child star are great additions to your life movies, but you don't want the child making the directorial decisions and rewriting the script. That's a job for the adult director.

If the adult is not present when you begin changing your script, the child is left to run things. The child wants to cling to the familiar habits and will keep sabotaging changes. The adult is motivated to change the script and to temper the change with wisdom, insight, and resourcefulness. The adult can play many roles—writer, director, and editor—and all have a function in script changes. This process is not a place for children; this movie is for adults only.

In this chapter, you will learn how to rewrite your old scripts. We will be focusing on how to change your beliefs, thoughts, and feelings. Briefly, the questions you will be asking yourself are these:
- What are my beliefs? Are they true?
- What are my thoughts? Are they rational?
- What are my feelings? Are they the feelings I want to have?
- What beliefs, thoughts, and feelings would work better for me?

Changing one thing will trigger a change in the others and, ultimately, will change your behavior. Later, in chapter eight, we will look at how you can change your behavior, even if your beliefs, thoughts, and feelings have not changed.

The Director's Challenge

The Director's Challenge is a conscious, analytical, mindful process you use to examine the elements of your scripts—your beliefs, thoughts, feelings, and behaviors—to see how they are linked. It gives you a way to dispute the negative parts of your script and create doubt about their truth and usefulness.

You can use the Director's Challenge in situations that stir up negative thoughts, bad feelings, inappropriate behaviors, or poor results. The process makes you aware of the automatic, unconscious responses you use and helps you replace them with positive, productive responses.

The Director's Challenge starts by challenging and disputing your scripts and, based on your current situation, identifying why they are no longer appropriate. It is a process that helps you stay in your head, not get lost in your emotions. It continues by looking for alternate ways of thinking, feeling, and responding. Rewriting your scripts takes place when you choose to think and feel differently. Your adult director looks for choices that best help further a successful plot and lead to better results.

In his book *Three-Minute Therapy*, Michael Edelstein offers two guiding principles to making script changes:

    1. Accept that you are responsible for your own emotions and actions.
    2. Recognize that your harmful emotions and behaviors are the products of your irrational thinking.

Let these guiding principles help you begin the process of rewriting your scripts. I also suggest keeping your goal in mind—to create success at work and have greater satisfaction in life. It will keep you motivated to make positive changes.

The Child Inside Will Resist

As you use the Director's Challenge to dispute your old scripts, the child inside you won't be happy. Like real children, your inner child is a force that doesn't like change and needs reassurance when you start trashing old scripts. To change, you have to deal with this powerful force, which is the same part of you that sabotages you from achieving success as an adult.

Staying in present time helps. By this, I mean staying in the adult mind. The fearful child worries about the future and obsesses about the past, a trick maneuver that keeps you from focusing on your current situation. When situations evoke memories and emotions from the past, you are thrown back into the child's mind. You have to recognize that yesterday is over—it's a *wrap* as they say in the movies. You can't rewrite it; you can't redo it. Similarly, the future isn't real either. It hasn't happened yet. Your anxiety about the future keeps you stuck because it makes you afraid to change. Stay in the here and now so you can rewrite your scripts for today's world.

Challenging Your Reactions

As discussed in the previous chapter, when you respond to an event, you go through a series of steps:

    • You perceive or interpret the event through the filter of your *belief system*.

- You have some ideas about your perception of the event. These are your *thoughts*.
- Your thoughts create *feelings*.
- Your feelings lead to actions, or *behavior*.

Your responses are almost always automatic and unconscious. You need to become conscious of your responses to intervene and change them.

You can step in at any point in the above process. Since each element flows into the next element, when you change one element, everything that follows also changes. When you change your belief system, you will find that your thoughts, feelings, and behavior change to be consistent with the new beliefs. You could also intervene at the point of feelings and change your negative feelings to positive ones. As your negative feelings change, your behavior changes.

At any point, you as the director can intervene and say, "Cut!" Cut to examine what you're experiencing. Cut at the belief-system point, and challenge your beliefs. Cut as you become aware of your thoughts and, challenge them. Cut when your feelings awaken, and examine and challenge what you feel. Cut when you do something, and stop to analyze your behavior.

When you use the Director's Challenge process, you call upon the very rational and logical parts of yourself. You want to look for objective evidence to support your findings. You use the objective eye of the camera to see what happens in your scenarios, and you draw upon the maturity and wisdom of the director to make changes.

Perceptions Can Change

Each scenario you encounter has multiple interpretations, and yours is just one. How you choose to perceive or interpret a situation is based on your belief system.

Derek and Aurelia were standing in Charlie's cubicle one morning discussing a project they were working on. All three looked up when their boss, Gwen, entered. She looked at Charlie and said, "Charlie, did you send that contract to Legal?"

"Yes, I sent it over yesterday."

Gwen nodded, then turned and headed toward her office. "Let me know when you get a response," she said as she walked away.

When Gwen left, Aurelia turned back to Charlie and continued their conversation. Derek didn't join in. He felt hurt and upset that Gwen didn't acknowledge him. Later that day, when Gwen solicited the group for ideas during a staff meeting, he didn't respond.

Let's look at Derek's process:

1. Event: Gwen approaches the group and does not say hello to me.
2. Perception: Gwen intentionally ignores me.
3. Thought: Gwen is angry at me. She must be disappointed with that status report I left on her desk.
4. Feeling: Hurt, worried.
5. Action: I withdraw from participating in the staff meeting when Gwen asks for suggestions.

Derek's perception is filtered through his belief system. He believes that when people don't acknowledge him, it's because they are angry at him. As a child, he observed his parents giving each other the silent treatment when they were angry at each other. He grew up believing this is how adults behave to show disapproval. Now he interprets Gwen's silence through his old belief.

Aurelia and Charlie interpreted the situation very differently, as Derek discovered. After the staff meeting, Aurelia said to Derek, "You were pretty quiet. Is something wrong?"

Derek explained his distress to Aurelia. "I think Gwen was ignoring me because she's mad at me," he said.

"Wait a minute," Aurelia said. "Gwen didn't say hello to me, either, but I don't think she was ignoring me. I think she's got so much on her mind that she's cruising in La-la-land."

"If Gwen's mad at anyone, it's me," Charlie said. "That contract was supposed to go to Legal last week, and I forgot to send it. Gwen had to remind me. Besides, I've noticed that sometimes when she's annoyed with one person, she's pretty surly to everybody."

Aurelia, Charlie, and Derek saw the situation differently because they filtered input through their individual belief systems. Aurelia believed that when people are distracted, they ignore others. Charlie may have beeen feeling a little guilty about his forgetfulness, but he did not believe Gwen was snubbing him.

Derek believed Gwen was angry at him and therefore snubbed him. As evidence, he remembered his parents' behavior when they were angry. Aurelia and Charlie's remarks helped Derek see there were other ways to interpret the event. Derek also did what so many people do: he assumed from his child mind that *he* caused someone's behavior. He saw himself as the star of *Derek's World* and didn't consider that he was just a bit player in *Gwen's World*!

When he interprets his situation using old evidence from the past, he feels in control of his thoughts. Aurelia and Charlie's different assessments of the situation prompt Derek to question his whole belief system. "Gee, if I am wrong about what Gwen's behavior meant, maybe I'm wrong about my parents' behavior, too. Maybe they *weren't* angry when they ignored each other. Maybe something else was going on." Now he feels he's lost control of his thoughts.

We maintain a fantasy that if we understand a situation we can control it or fix it. When Derek's parents gave each other the silent treatment, Derek felt woeful and neglected. He would fix the situation for himself by withdrawing to his room to indulge in his childish feelings of self-pity. He still does the same thing today. When he thinks he's being ignored, he feels sad and hurt. He withdraws by not participating in things at work, and he feels sorry for himself.

When Aurelia and Charlie's comments give Derek a new understanding, he has to change his thoughts, and in turn his feelings and behavior. He can no longer fume about Gwen being mad at him, and he can no longer feel sorry for himself. Instead, he has an opportunity to choose new, adult reactions more appropriate for the situation. He can choose to believe Gwen is not angry at him. He can ask her what she thinks of the report instead of guessing. The new interpretation frees Derek from wasting time feeling sorry for himself and acting like a victim.

To continue to grow and develop, we must continuously challenge our beliefs and keep asking if they still serve us. The world changes; the workplace changes; we change. In childhood, we believed in the Tooth Fairy. Other beliefs we cling to are just as childish as the Tooth Fairy myth and much more dangerous to hold on to.

You Can Challenge and Dispute Your Perceptions

To execute a useful challenge, you first need to detach from a situation to see it from a different perspective. Detaching dilutes the intensity of your reactions so you can see things objectively. Talking to someone else, as Derek did, helps you detach through different perspectives.

Watch out for the tendency to seek conversation only with people who share your views. Sometimes you may think you're asking for another reaction or interpretation when you really want someone to reassure you that you are right—the role of a classic Hollywood yes-man! It will be most helpful for you to talk to someone who has a different interpretation.

The camera lens approach we discussed earlier is another way to detach. The camera is an objective observer of the event and records only the facts of the situation—what was said and done—and the order in which things happened. So pull back and imagine yourself being the cinematographer looking though the lens to film the scene. As you do that, ask yourself the following questions:

- What do I think has happened?
- What evidence do I have that my interpretation is accurate?
- What evidence do I have that my interpretation is inaccurate?
- What is another way to interpret the situation?

Each time you encounter life situations that leave you feeling confused or uncomfortable, challenge your interpretation. Detach and look at the situation from a distance. Try to see it through the lens of a camera and ask yourself the four questions above.

Movies of the Mind

In chapter one, you identified some of your own beliefs. Being able to link your beliefs to your thoughts, feelings, and behaviors is important because it's a way for you to understand why you do the things you do—or *don't* do the things you want to do.

We create our view of reality based on our beliefs. Yet that reality and the scenarios we imagine are really just movies of the mind. They are projections of how we think life should be, not how life is. This is an important concept to remember.

Your beliefs can be invisible to you. They are so integrated into your old scripts that it can be hard to identify them and yank them out for examination. Sometimes you aren't even aware of what your beliefs are until you encounter someone with a different belief system. Like most people, you probably think of your beliefs as reality. When you're with someone with a conflicting belief system, you likely think that person is wrong. You may even think, "Well, that may work for *you*, but it sure won't work for *me*."

Your beliefs run you. Yet, most people rarely question their beliefs. When you don't question your scripts, you don't fully realize that you could write a better one.

I once had a client who said, "Misery chooses me." She believed life was full of pain and suffering and that she wasn't supposed to be happy.

"You have a choice here to do things differently," I told her. "Misery is optional; suffering is optional."

Her eyes narrowed. "Do you think I *want* to feel this way? I don't want to be miserable!"

No, consciously she didn't want to be miserable, but unconsciously she continuously chose to stew in depressing thoughts and miserable feelings. They were consistent with her belief system. When she watched the news on television, she focused only on the bad news stories. She chose to pay attention to the negative stories that supported her belief that life was miserable. She could spin wild fantasies and create elaborate scenarios that would make any melodrama or disaster movie look pale in comparison, but doing this only increased her suffering. None of these mental movies were real, but they still possessed the power to keep her trapped.

Sometimes we think that our beliefs are part of our hard wiring. Actually, you weren't born with them; you created them. As we discussed in chapter one, beliefs are not genetic; they are learned. Some things you believe were never true; they were someone else's fear or myth, and you incorporated them into your belief system.

Beliefs are neither good nor bad, but they can have a positive or a negative effect on your life. When they limit you or are blueprints for pain, you can change them, creating blueprints for success and happiness. You had the power to create your beliefs in the first place; you still have the power to re-create them. You can rewrite them—or re-right them!

Limiting Beliefs

The negative beliefs about yourself, such as "I'm not good enough," "I'm not deserving," "I'm worthless," "I'm stupid," or "I can't do it," have the power to limit you and prevent you from fulfilling your potential in any endeavor, especially when you're faced with difficult, uncomfortable, or unfamiliar situations.

Other self-limiting beliefs—"I'm too young," "I'm too old," "I can't learn," "I worry what others will think," "I want everyone to like me," and "I'm afraid other people will hurt me"—keep you stuck in childhood roles.

Generalized negative beliefs about work and jobs affect your success. These beliefs include "ambitious people are stupid," "making lots of money is evil," "work isn't supposed to be fun," "it's my manager's job to tell me what to do," "women/Blacks/Latinos/Asians/gays can never get ahead," and "employees have no power."

Some beliefs can make it difficult to accept and deal with change. These include, "change is bad," "change always brings trouble," "it's management's job to make this work," and "it's all going to change again, so why should I care?"

The voice we imagine intoning these negative beliefs is the voice of the critic. It's the voice of an internalized, judgmental parent pressuring you to remain trapped in the role of a powerless child. Breaking out of the child's role means fighting back with an adult voice. To develop that adult voice, you need to assume the role of the director and challenge these insidious beliefs propagated by the internal critic.

You can create tremendous misery when you make unreasonable demands on yourself, others, and the universe at large. Michael Edelstein calls such demands the "musts." In *Three-Minute Therapy*, he identifies three core *musts*. They are:

1. A *must* about yourself, such as, "I must do well or else I'm worthless."
2. A *must* about others, such as, "You must like me or else you're no good."
3. A *must* about the universe, such as, "Life must be fair or else it's awful."

These *musts* are irrational beliefs. Booting them from your life is a big step in relieving yourself of emotional distress. You can use the Director's Challenge to dispute these self-defeating musts.

Challenge and Dispute Self-Limiting Beliefs

Andy, the manager in the research firm, has the self-limiting belief, "I'm not okay if I'm not perfect." He feels gut-wrenching anxiety when forced to make a critical decision because he is terrified of making the wrong one. I worked with Andy to help him challenge his belief and dispute its validity. He recalled a recent situation when he had to make a decision and was paralyzed by his belief.

I first asked him where his belief had come from. He said his parents were very exacting people, and they harshly criticized him if they felt he turned in a poor performance. He came to believe that nothing less than perfection would make him acceptable to his parents. "I believed then that I must be perfect, and I guess I still believe it very strongly today. On a scale of one to ten, I'd rate my belief a ten."

I asked Andy what evidence he had to support his belief. He was silent for a moment, and then said, "I really have no objective evidence—just what my parents taught me. My father always said 'If it's worth doing, it's worth doing well' and 'If it's not done right, it's not done at all.' He meant well, but he was very demanding. I think my father probably said these things because his father had said them. My father had very high standards for himself, too, but he seemed to be unhappy most of the time."

Andy realized he was afraid to make a wrong decision because he was trying to live up to his father's standards. He had inherited his belief from his father and had accepted it without question. I asked him to question the belief now by looking for evidence that it was false. Again, he sat silent for a moment. Then he said, "I've turned in reports or completed projects that were not up to my perfectionist standards, but my manager and other people were happy with my work."

I asked him to think about how his belief served his goals for success and what it would cost him at work if he continued to hold on to this belief. "My belief doesn't serve me," Andy said. "It holds me back and makes it difficult for me to be productive and make decisions. If I hold on to it, I'll continue to struggle, agonize, and be anxious every time I have to make a decision."

Finally, I asked Andy to identify the new self-enhancing belief he wanted to have. He took a deep breath and then said, "I am a bright, capable person. I trust when I do my best, the results will be successful. I am not my work." He repeated these statements again as if to impress them in his memory. I asked how strongly he still believed his old belief now. He smiled and said, "It's not as strong now. It's about a five."

By challenging and disputing his self-limiting belief, Andy was able to replace it with new, productive and positive beliefs. As we worked together, he learned to use the Director's Challenge by himself to dispute other self-limiting beliefs and rewrite his scripts.

Changing Your Self-Limiting Beliefs

You can use the Director's Challenge to dispute and change your self-limiting beliefs. Go back to exercise 4-A in chapter four on page 94 where you identified an upsetting situation at work that is creating discomfort for you. Use this situation for the following exercises or, if you prefer, select something that has recently upset you at work. Ask yourself the following questions:

1. What is your self-limiting belief or assumption in this situation?

2. On a scale of 1 to 10, how strong is your belief? (A rating of 1 means "I don't believe it at all;" a 10 means "I completely believe it.")

3. Where did your belief or assumption come from?

4. As you think about this situation, what emotion do you experience? Where do you feel the emotion? Is your stomach upset, does your head hurt, is your jaw tense?

5. On a scale of 1 to 10, how intense is the feeling? (A rating of 1 means "not intense;" and 10 means, "very intense.")

6. What evidence do you have that your self-limiting belief or assumption is true?

7. If the evidence comes from something another person told you, who is that person? Can you trust how this person arrived at this belief?

8. What evidence do you have that this belief is false? (Dig deeply here. The evidence may not be readily apparent because we try to block out things that don't agree with our beliefs.)

9. How does this belief serve your goals for success?

10. How does holding this belief enhance your life?

11. What will it cost you at work if you continue to hold on to this belief?

12. What new self-enhancing belief do you want to have?

13. Thinking about the event again, and with new understanding that you can change your self-limiting belief or assumption, on a scale of 1 to 10, how intense is the event now?

14. On a scale of 1 to 10, how strongly do you believe your belief or assumption is true?

With practice, this number will go down, and you will feel less upset and distressed. Your old negative beliefs are faulty and irrational. Toss them out and replace them with positive, successful beliefs.

The Beliefs That Work Best in the Workplace

In addition to changing negative personal beliefs that hold you back, you also want to challenge limiting beliefs you have about work and success. You need a set of positive, empowering beliefs for the workplace and for *My Successful Career*. The beliefs should support the characteristics managers seek and the new mindset that represents the reality of today's workplace.

The following beliefs relating to the realities of today's workplace lead to success:

Change management
- Change brings opportunities.
- I can manage change.
- I enjoy new challenges.

Entrepreneurial attitude
- I'm willing to take risks.
- There is more than one way to do things.
- I can make my own decisions. I can make appropriate choices.
- I take responsibility for my behavior.
- I take responsibility for the part I play in solving problems.
- If I make a poor decision, I can deal with the consequences competently.
- Making a mistake or a poor decision does not mean I'm a failure. Mistakes are opportunities to learn and grow.
- I see opportunities wherever I look.

Collaboration and teamwork
- There is power in teams. We are all in this together.
- I am committed to my team's success.
- My teammates and co-workers deserve respect.
- Not everyone has to like me for us to work together.
- I can ask for support from my team members, and I can support them.
- I interact well with internal and external clients.
- I am an effective communicator.
- I can confront difficult issues with people at work in a positive and constructive manner.

Optimism
- I am okay; I am capable; I am competent.
- I am self-motivated, self-directed, and self-reliant.

- I can learn; I have resources to draw on.
- Everything will turn out fine.
- I can solve it. I can figure it out.
- I can set my own limits and boundaries.
- I am persistent and continue working toward my goals despite setbacks.
- I work with clarity of purpose to attain my goals.

Career self-management
- I am in charge of my career.
- I can see opportunities to further my growth and development.

Additional beliefs for managers and leaders:
- I am fair, consistent, and open-minded.
- I do not have to be liked.
- I earn respect and trust.

Taking Things Personally

Nora throws tantrums and verbally assaults people who don't follow her advice. She personalizes every situation she's in. Several months ago she was asked to consult with a company whose customer data had been accessed by someone from the outside. She conducted her usual careful study of the situation and developed a plan of action for the company to make its systems and data secure. However, despite the company's insistence that information security is one of their top priorities, Nora recently has discovered that her action plan still has not been fully implemented.

Nora takes the company's lapse personally. The situation triggers her negative beliefs, "If people don't do what I recommend, I'm wrong" and "I'm not okay." She believes the company does not value her advice and that they think she is incompetent. She is convinced that she is the real reason the company has not followed the action plan she prepared. It doesn't occur to her that the company has other reasons for its decision. As it turns out, the manager in charge of implementing the plan left the company, and no one has taken charge of the assignment.

Nora personalizes the situation in yet another way; she feels personally responsible for the risks the company takes in not implementing her plan. She's afraid that if a security breach occurs, she'll be blamed. This fear drives her to defend herself, and she does this by accusing the client of being careless. Her attack is also fueled by her rage about being ignored, just as she was ignored as a child.

If Nora chose instead to believe that she's okay and that the company's decision had nothing to do with her personally, the fear and anger would subside. She would be able to look at the situation in a rational, objective light. This would also help her understand that, as a consultant, she can advise clients, but she can't force them to follow her advice.

Some people perceive everything bad that happens at work in very personal terms, just as Nora does. If you personalize each experience, you'll interpret the accidental push in the elevator as a deliberate shove because of who you are. You'll think, "They pushed me because of my gender/race/religion/sexual preference/looks/size." You'll believe that people are out to conspire to prevent you from being successful. When you personalize each situation like this, you're choosing to foist yourself into the center arena of every bad situation and believe it all revolves around you.

People who regularly personalize bad situations have basic negative beliefs about themselves. They think they are not okay and that something is wrong with them. They also have negative beliefs about others: people don't like me; people want to hurt me; people are conspiring against me.

Ask yourself: Do you want to hurt other people? Do you plot with others to hurt someone? I'm sure the answer is *no*, because most people do not hurt others intentionally. If you are not out to hurt others, why do you think they are out to hurt you?

Using the Director's Challenge from exercise 5-A on pages 116–17 to dispute your basic negative beliefs will stop the pattern of personalizing. You will also benefit by asking yourself the following questions:

- What if I choose to believe I am okay?
- What if I choose to believe that what other people do is not about me?
- What if I choose to believe that this person is not doing this to hurt me?

When you choose to believe positive things about yourself and others, you will interpret bad situations in a new light. When you choose to believe other people are not out to hurt you, you won't feel hurt.

You Can Change Your Thoughts

When you dispute and change your beliefs, your thoughts will start to change. However, you can also challenge and dispute your negative, unproductive thoughts directly and replace them with positive, productive thoughts.

Challenging her thoughts helped Miranda change her reactions in an awkward situation. Miranda met with her manager, Albert, to review the status of a project to upgrade the workstations in the customer service center. She was in the middle of explaining that the implementation date had to be pushed out because one vendor would be unable to deliver all of the equipment on time. "This is a disaster," Albert interrupted. "We've promised to have these workstations up and running on time. I was counting on you to make this project run smoothly. If it doesn't . . . well . . ." He paused for a moment, then continued, describing the impact the delay would have not only on the service center but also on his department's credibility and his own reputation.

As soon as Albert started speaking, Miranda began to feel terrible. Although it wasn't her fault that the vendor couldn't deliver on time, she took responsibility for letting Albert down. Quickly, a barrage of negative thoughts filled her head: "He's right. This *is* a disaster. It's my fault. How could I let this happen? He should never have put me in charge of this project. I don't know what I'm doing. I'm a big disappointment."

I had been coaching Miranda on how to change the way she responded to other people's criticism and anger. She had learned that if she continued thinking in this self-sabotaging vein, she would increase her feelings of incompetence and exasperate Albert with her helpless reaction. She had to turn her thoughts and feelings around immediately. This was the perfect situation to apply the concepts we had been working with.

Then Miranda said to herself, "Cut!" She took a deep breath to settle herself, and she sat up straight. She thought about what the situation reminded her of from the past. "I'm feeling like a little girl," she thought. "I feel as if I've done something horribly wrong, and now I have to pay for it. I'm making my body smaller in my chair. I'm dropping my head down, hunching my shoulders, and breathing in little shallow breaths. This is just the way I felt and acted when I was a little girl and my mother yelled at me for something I'd done."

Then she thought, "I'm not a child anymore; I'm an adult. I have to think and act like an adult. I'm mature, I'm capable, I can solve things. I have to focus on Albert's concerns and how we can solve this problem."

Miranda very quickly went through a Director's Challenge to change her thoughts and feelings. She noticed what her negative thoughts were: "It's my fault. I'm a big disappointment." She recalled a situation from her childhood when she had similar thoughts while being reprimanded by her mother. She recognized her body was in a childhood pose. When she thought "Cut!" she stopped the negative thoughts from consuming her, and she stopped the negative feelings from overpowering her. Taking a deep breath caused her body to shift slightly and helped her detach from the intensity of her feelings. She stayed focused on the present situation and replaced the negative thoughts with positive, self-affirming thoughts.

Miranda did not let her child steal the show. She stayed in her adult mind and focused on the present instead of the past. This made it possible for her to listen carefully to Albert, cope with his feelings of anxiety, and move them both into a constructive problem-solving mode. By the end of the meeting, they had worked out a way to revise the project to handle the vendor's limitations while still satisfying the service center and preserving their department's credibility. Miranda left the meeting feeling good about herself and the project, not powerless, incompetent, and wishing she worked somewhere else.

Change Your Thoughts on the Spot

Just as Miranda did, you can use the Director's Challenge whenever negative thoughts fill your mind and create negative feelings. Do the following:

1. Say "Cut!" when the negative thoughts pop up. Stay in present time, focused on where you are at the moment.
2. Make a conscious effort to freeze or stop the thoughts.
3. Take a deep breath. Change your body position.
4. Detach and step into the director's place to examine the thoughts rationally and objectively.
5. Ask yourself these questions:
- What am I thinking?
- Are my thoughts productive? Will they help me get what I want?
- What thoughts do I want to have about myself or about this situation?

Miranda took a deep breath when she began the Director's Challenge. I suggest you do the same. The breathing helps in two ways. First, it creates

Scenarios for Success

Camera

Changing Your Negative Thoughts

Exercise # 5 - B

Use the Director's Challenge to challenge and change your negative thoughts. You can use the situation from exercise 4-A in chapter four on page 94, or if you prefer, think of a recent situation at work that has stirred up negative thoughts. Recall the situation in detail, then detach and step into the director's place to challenge your thoughts objectively. Answer the following questions.

- What are my thoughts?

- What does this situation remind me of from my past?

- Am I using the same thoughts from my past?

- Are these thoughts rational? What evidence supports that they are rational?

- Are they productive? Will they help me get what I want?

- What thoughts do I want to have about myself or about this situation?

energy and helps you relax. Negative feelings often enervate and deplete us. Second, breathing deeply makes you stand up or sit up straight, as an adult. Recall that Miranda became aware she was shrinking in her chair, hunching her shoulders and dropping her head to her chest. This is the body posture of a hurt child or a victim.

When you take a deep breath, you cause your body to change position. This alone often dilutes the intensity of the feelings. It's nearly impossible to think, "I'm all alone, a poor victim," when you sit up or stand up straight, put your shoulders back, hold your head high, and look straight ahead. Note the body postures of people at work who are successful and appear to be full of self-confidence. You'll see that they appear comfortable and at ease in their bodies.

You Can Change Your Feelings

Changing your thoughts will have an immediate impact on your feelings because upsetting feelings come from upsetting thoughts. If you keep repeating the upsetting thoughts, you will stay upset. You can even reactivate upsetting feelings by remembering—or replaying in your mind—a disturbing scene from the past. That's how people keep their bad feelings burning for years. They rerun *Highlights From My Worst Moments* in excruciating detail. Each memory refreshes unpleasant thoughts that, in turn, rekindle negative feelings.

You can test this connection between thoughts and feelings right now. First, think of a time when you were angry. Maybe it was as recently as yesterday, when a droning telemarketer called and forced you to miss the best part of your favorite television show. Maybe it was when you were a child and your parents wouldn't buy you the one toy you desperately wanted—or when you were a teenager and they grounded you for a week. Recall the scene in detail, playing it back in your mind as if you were watching a movie. What did the other person say or do? What did you say or do?

As you relive the scene and recall the angry thoughts, notice how you start to feel angry again. You weren't feeling angry until you thought about the scene, but as soon as you focus on it, the anger returns. The more you think about it, the angrier you can get. In fact, you could work yourself into quite a lather by focusing on that scene.

Now do this: think about a pleasant memory and a time when you felt happy or pleased. You might remember a compliment from someone, or how your child looked as a baby smiling for the first time. Again, re-create the scene in your mind in detail, just as if you were watching a film. What happened in the scene? What did you and others say and do? As you think about the scene, the positive feelings associated with the memory come floating back. If you really focus on that pleasant memory, the feelings of anger you evoked just a minute ago should go away, replaced by the good feelings. Pleasant and positive thoughts create good feelings.

Is it really that simple? If you think happy thoughts every time you have bad feelings, can you make your bad feelings go away? Well, no, it's not quite that simple at first. You have to challenge and dispute the negative thoughts actively before you can replace them with positive thoughts. However, if you continue to do this, you'll learn how to challenge quickly. Eventually you will reach the point where you can say, "Cut! I don't want to wallow in misery. I want to feel better."

You Can Flip Back and Forth Between Feelings

You can focus on only one thought and one feeling at a time. It's just like what happens when you have one object close at hand and another object in the distance. You can't focus on both at the same time. When you focus on one, the other is blurred. You have to flip back and forth between them, focusing first on one, then on another. The same thing happens with your thoughts and feelings.

Sometimes people say, "I feel happy and sad at the same time." Actually, they are not experiencing both feelings at the same time—they are flipping back and forth between conflicting thoughts and feelings. You can be happy you got the new job and sad you'll be leaving your friends at the old one. You flip back and forth between two different thoughts that stimulate two different feelings.

If you did the experiment above with activating feelings of anger and happiness, you can experience the alternative flashes. When you focus on being interrupted by a droning telemarketer, you feel angry. When you focus on a baby's smile, you feel happy. It's your choice. Do you want to focus on good thoughts and feelings or bad ones?

Preparing to Handle Bad Feelings

Sometimes you know in advance that you'll be facing a situation that could easily trigger negative thoughts or uncomfortable feelings. Miranda probably knows from working with Albert that he does not take bad news well. She knows that she feels diminished and childlike when she hears his comments. You have probably gone to meetings that you knew beforehand could turn out to be unpleasant.

You can prepare yourself in advance for these situations by jotting down several positive self-affirming thoughts. Keep them handy. Bring the list with you or keep it in the forefront of your mind so you can refer to it quickly when the negative thoughts start flowing. Resolve to stay in present time instead of letting your thoughts slip back into the murky past.

Some people may welcome criticism; most of us don't. Like Miranda, with her initial reactions to Albert's criticism, we often feel diminished and thrust back into the child's role, reacting to bigger, stronger parents. It's like beaming into a completely different mental state. Our responses can range from feeling small and helpless to crying, pouting, or even attacking the other person.

As a child, you didn't have control. You responded from your base emotions. As an adult, you need to understand that criticism can be valuable feedback, not an attack or diminution of who you are. Staying in a present-time adult role will help you listen to the other person, to separate the message from the individual—who may not be very good at delivering criticism—and to extract the value from his or her comments.

Change Your Feelings on the Spot

Just as you can change your negative thoughts on the spot, you can challenge and change your negative feelings on the spot. In fact, the process is the same.

Here are the steps to follow to change your negative or uncomfortable feelings.

1. Say "Cut!" when you become aware of the feeling. This keeps you in the logical, rational adult mind and prevents the emotional child star from taking over.
2. Take a couple of deep breaths.
3. Detach from the scene by imagining you are watching the situation through a camera lens. This different perspective also helps dilute the intensity of your feeling and clears your mind so you can analyze the situation and choose more appropriate feelings.
4. Ask yourself these questions:
   - What am I feeling?
   - Is this how I want to feel right now? Is this feeling productive?
   - How do I want to feel?

Transfer Your Feelings

Another way to change your feelings instantly is to transfer positive feelings from another experience to your present situation. Here's how:

Recall a time when you felt very successful about something you were doing and very positive about yourself. Flash back to that experience and examine it in detail. Remember how it felt to be successful, capable, and confident. Focus on those positive feelings. Finally, think of a mental picture you can use to invoke that scene and those feelings quickly.

Carmela re-entered the work force after fifteen years of raising a large family. She took a position as an administrative assistant in a small legal firm. She told me she felt intimidated by the five attorneys in the firm, particularly when they all demanded she do something for them at the same time. She struggled to meet their needs, while feeling as if she were far beneath the challenges of the job.

I asked Carmela to remember a time when she *had* felt competent and successful. She replied she had felt successful handling all the demands of running a household with four active children. She described the difficulty of trying to please all five attorneys gathered around her desk like a wolf pack, each waving a briefcase full of papers at her. It reminded her of her four children clustered around her waving their school work and demanding her attention all at the same time. I suggested that she imagine the attorneys' briefcases turning into colorful lunch boxes and their legal briefs turning into homework.

The next day in the office, whenever the attorneys approached her desk with their demands, she pictured them holding lunch boxes instead of briefcases, and her feelings of intimidation lessened. Whenever she began to feel intimidated and overwhelmed at work, she would use the colorful lunch-box metaphor to reframe the situation and feel her success. She transferred her competencies at home to the office.

If you can remember a time you felt successful and good about yourself, you can counter the negative thoughts and feelings you experience by transferring those positive thoughts from the past to the present.

Acting on Your Feelings

Many people act inappropriately, then use their feelings as a rationale or excuse for their behavior: "I was so angry, I had to say something." "I couldn't help it; he made me feel like a child." "I was scared, so I panicked and left." When you let feelings run you, you let the tail wag the dog. Actually, the child wags, or controls, the adult.

Nora, the information security consultant, lets her feelings rule her. When an interaction with clients or staff goes against her belief of how it should be, strong negative feelings of hurt, anger, or shame pour out. Nora is like an emotional volcano. Under stress, she blows up. The intensity of her reaction is way out of proportion to the severity of the situation. She ends up resembling the tantrum-throwing child she once was.

Strong negative feelings need to be dealt with. If you don't acknowledge and identify them, you may behave inappropriately.

Often my clients will describe a situation and the bad feelings resulting from it. When I ask them if there's another way they could feel, many look at me with bewilderment. "Wouldn't anyone feel this way?" they ask, not realizing that they choose their feelings. You decide if you want the feelings you have and then choose the feelings you want to have.

Feelings are funny: if you try to ignore them or conceal them, they express themselves in other ways. You've heard the phrase, "The best defense is a good offense." Some people take this to heart and handle their feelings of inadequacy by being belligerent or putting others down with sarcastic remarks. They're hiding their true feelings of inadequacy by "copping an attitude." A more appropriate way is to acknowledge your feelings, accept them, find out where they came from, and replace them with positive feelings. Feelings aren't right or wrong. What's wrong is to ignore your feelings, let them control you, and then let the feelings lead to behavior that causes you and others pain.

Many of us would prefer to have someone else attend to our feelings. We would like to experience the comfort we felt when our parents healed our woes as children. We look to our mates or our managers to do this for us, yet it's our responsibility to attend to our own feelings.

Your thoughts and beliefs reside in your head, but your feelings reside in your body. You may not always be able to identify the feeling or collection of feelings you're experiencing, but you can readily identify the body sensations:

- Knots or butterflies in the stomach
- Tension in the jaw or shoulders
- A pounding heart
- Feeling flushed
- Shallow breathing
- Tightness in the chest

You are not your feelings. You give your feelings control over your responses. Think of your negative feelings—anger, hurt, sadness, disappointment—as a breeze wafting over you. The breeze comes and goes. It's the same with your feelings; they come and go. They're always in a transitory state; they are not who you are. You can change them, often within an instant.

Scenarios for Success

Changing Your Feelings

Camera

Exercise # | 5 - C

As you dispute and change your beliefs and thoughts, your feelings will change. However, regardless of what your beliefs and thoughts are, you can still change your feelings when they're not the feelings you want.

Recall a recent uncomfortable situation at work when you felt powerless, ineffective, or incapable. As you recall the situation and re-experience the feeling, detach and step into the director's place to examine your feelings rationally and objectively. Answer the following questions.

- What am I feeling?

- What does this situation remind me of from my past?

- Am I experiencing the same feelings from my past?

- Are the feelings I have now rational? What is the evidence that they are rational?

- Are they productive? Will they help me get what I want?

- What feelings do I want to have about myself or about this situation?

You Can Always Choose

You can always choose what you want to believe, think, and how you want to feel. No event or situation—no matter how unpleasant—and no person—no matter how compelling—can force you to believe, think or feel a certain way. If you don't accept this you are choosing to be controlled by your beliefs, thoughts, and feelings and those people capable of eliciting a response from you.

Many of us watch our heroes in the movies and vicariously enjoy their power. Our heroes often display incredible courage, astounding ingenuity, awesome stamina, a deep love of life, a fast wit. They usually meet obstacles head on, even when they suffer enormously; and we love watching them succeed. They always seem to know what to say at just the right time, yet we often leave the movie theater thinking, "But it was just a movie. Of course they know what to say at the right time. Some guy got paid fifty thousand dollars to write the script!"

But you really *can* take creative control of your life in the way that a movie-making team takes creative control of a motion picture. You can become the most heroic, adventurous, successful figure you can imagine. You have to learn how to use your own creative ability to choose the beliefs, thoughts, and feelings you want to have. It takes practice; it doesn't happen overnight. But the more you practice, the better you get. With every successful episode in which you turn negative feelings around, you'll become more confident in your creative abilities.

Life is a precious gift, and too often we wait until it is too late before we take action. Take a few minutes to think about how you would answer these questions:

- If this were your last day on Earth, what *beliefs* would you choose to have about yourself and about others?
- If this were your last day on Earth, what *thoughts* would you choose to have about yourself and about others?
- If this were your last day on Earth, how would you choose to *feel*?
- How would you choose to spend your last day on Earth?

Happily, you don't have to wait until your last day on Earth to have the beliefs, thoughts, and feelings you want to have.

Chapter 6

Award-Winning Optimism
Shifting Your Focus

When you reflect on your favorite film characters, you most likely find that you prefer characters who make something happen. They are the ones who keep moving no matter what life hurls at them. They look for ingenious ways to solve their problems, whether those solutions are physical or mental. Your favorite characters are undefeated in the face of adversity. They don't throw their hands up in despair, fall down in a heap at the first sign of trouble, and complain throughout the rest of the picture.

In this chapter, we look at optimism and pessimism. I think of these as lenses through which we view life and that, as you will see, have a tremendous impact on success in the workplace. The characters that you like in the movies—the ones who make things happen—are the optimists.

Two Views of a Situation

One morning during a staff meeting, Rhonda and Martin's supervisor announced, "Well, folks, the rumors are true. Senior management has decided to outsource our group. As a result, our department will be closed at the end of this month. You'll each be given a generous severance package and outplacement counseling to help you find new jobs."

Rhonda's spirit sank when she heard this news. "I can't believe it," she thought. "How can they do this to me after twenty years of loyal service?"

As soon as she could, Rhonda escaped to her office and closed the door. She sat by herself for an hour, not moving, as feelings of fright, anger, and despair engulfed her. Finally, she emerged from her office and went to see her supervisor. She asked if she could leave early because she wasn't feeling well.

On her way out, she ran into her colleague, Martin. "What's wrong, Rhonda? You don't look good."

"I feel terrible. This is the worst thing that could happen to me!"

"What?" Martin said calmly. "You mean getting laid off?"

"How am I supposed to find a new job?" Rhonda cried. "I'm almost forty-five years old. Nobody wants to hire people over forty!"

"Rhonda, relax! It's not the end of the world. I'm sure we'll both find great jobs somewhere else. Hey, we both have a lot to offer. I've just passed fifty—that's not old! This could be a chance to try something new and different. Or maybe we could even start our own consulting business."

"Yeah. Right," Rhonda said bitterly and walked away.

Your Lens Affects Your View

We have already seen how two people can have two completely different responses to the same event because each person filters the experience through the lens of his or her personal belief system. We use another lens, too—the lens of pessimism or optimism. When you explain the things that happen to you in a way that is a positive affirmation, it is optimism. It is pessimism when you put a negative spin on those events.

Optimism and pessimism are powerful lenses that affect your views of yourself, the world, and the things that happen to you. As with other thoughts in your belief system, pessimism is so pervasive and powerful that often you don't recognize it for what it is: *one way* of looking at the world. It is not the truth; it is simply one way to think. Unfortunately, pessimism limits your accomplishments and holds you back from being successful.

Looking at the world through the optimistic lens doesn't mean becoming a Pollyanna figure who ignores problems and perpetually thinks, "Gee, everything is wonderful!" Nor does it mean chanting a litany of positive affirmations to block out negative thoughts. Rather, it means choosing a hopeful, positive way of perceiving and explaining the things that happen in our lives.

A little verse by McLundburgh Wilson cleverly summarizes the difference between the outlooks of a pessimistic and an optimistic thinker:

Twixt the optimist and the pessimist,
The difference is droll.
The optimist sees the doughnut,
But the pessimist sees the hole.

It's the classic question: Is the glass half full or half empty? Your answer depends on your outlook on life. Neither answer is better. The person who answers half full is an optimist, while the person who responds half empty is a pessimist.

Your Outlook Affects Your Success

Professionals in behavioral science have found that one's outlook on life has a big impact on the success one achieves. The power of positive thinking has long been touted as a key to success, and studies confirm that optimistic people are generally more successful and happier in the workplace. They have a favorable outlook on life, expect things to go their way, and tend to be better at solving problems. They handle stress better than their pessimist co-workers, have fewer stress-related symptoms—headaches, tension, and fatigue—and enjoy better health. In one study of college students, pessimists were sick twice as many days as optimists. In addition, depression is much more likely to plague pessimists.

A study of the people who ran for political office found that the winners laced their speeches with optimistic language. The positive, can-do approach expressed in their speeches apparently appealed to voters, who rewarded them with votes.

Success is not so much what happens to you, but how you interpret those events. Your thinking propels you forward to great achievements and happiness or holds you prisoner in a rut of chronic misery.

Does optimism succeed in the workplace? Martin E. P. Seligman, a professor of psychology at the University of Pennsylvania, conducted extensive studies on the power of optimistic and pessimistic thinking. In one study, he surveyed the sales representatives of a large life insurance company to measure the impact of optimism and pessimism under adversity. The extremely optimistic insurance agents who believed they would be successful sold 88 percent more than the sales reps with extremely pessimistic attitudes.

Seligman's work has had a major impact in helping people in the face of adversity to alleviate their depression and to become successful. When I work with clients, I draw heavily on the information Seligman presents in his book *Learned Optimism*. When my pessimistic clients under coaching have used principles of optimistic thinking to deal with bad situations, I've seen them bounce out of slumps and quickly recover from disappointments.

Seligman's research, which I summarize in this chapter, led him to conclude that we are not born with an optimistic or pessimistic outlook. Instead, we learn to adopt an outlook according to how we were raised. Optimistic thinkers tend to have optimistic parents, while pessimistic thinkers tend to have pessimistic parents.

Children sometimes change that pattern when they rebel against their parents' pessimistic thinking, just as they rebel against other beliefs and attitudes their parents hold. Joel, for example, grew up seeing in his family how destructive pessimistic thinking could be. One time he raced home from his fourth-grade class to tell his mother that he had won an award at school for a semester of perfect attendance. His mother smiled and said , "Well, that's nice, but don't be disappointed if you don't win it next semester. There's a bad flu going around, you know. You're bound to get sick sometime this year."

Another time he brought home a report card with a C in algebra. His father launched into a long lecture about how this poor grade could prevent Joel from getting into college, finding a decent job, and making something of himself.

As Joel matured, he could see that his parents were unhappy and depressed most of the time, and he didn't want to end up like them. He didn't like how their pessimism diminished the pride he felt in his accomplishments and blew the mistakes he made out of proportion. He promised himself to put a more positive spin on the things that happened to him. Joel's optimistic outlook, which led him to become a highly successful investment advisor, was a reaction to his parents' crippling pessimism.

We develop either an optimistic or pessimistic way of thinking based on our childhood experiences. This thinking becomes part of our belief system, and it gets written into our scripts. While you may use a different way of thinking at times, one way of thinking usually predominates and becomes the habitual way you explain why good and bad situations happen.

Like Joel, even if you were raised in a household where pessimistic thinking reigned, you can still learn to think optimistically. Just as you learned how to change your beliefs, thoughts, and feelings, you can also learn how to reframe a pessimistic outlook.

How We Explain Good and Bad Events

When something happens to us, we evaluate the situation and explain why it happened. Seligman's research showed that people's explanations fit three categories: time, scope, and cause. I'll describe these categories briefly, then compare how an optimistic thinker and a pessimistic thinker explain good and bad events in their lives.

The *time* category refers to how long you believe the event or the effect of the event will last. Do you believe it is temporary—just for today or just this morning? Or do you believe it is permanent and will last a long time, maybe even forever?

Scope refers to what you believe is the extent or reach of the event. Do you believe the scope is specific, affecting just one area of your life? Or do you believe the scope is global and pervasive, with an impact on many areas of your life?

Cause refers to what you believe caused the event or made it occur. Do you believe the cause is internal or personal, that you alone made it happen? Or do you believe the cause is external, that other people or outside factors made it happen?

Interwoven into the category of cause are control and ownership issues. *Control* refers to how much power you believe you have in a situation. Do you have some control, at least control over your responses? Or do you believe you have no control, that there is nothing you can do? *Ownership* refers to owning the situation. If it's a bad situation, do you take ownership for the solution, instead of blaming yourself for the problem? If it's a good situation, do you believe you own the success?

Pessimists own the problem. When something bad happens, they go into self-blame. They think they created what happened because of what they did or who they are—"a terrible person." Feeling that they have no control, it's extremely difficult for pessimists to believe they can change or fix the situation. They feel a deep sense of helplessness.

Optimists own the solution. They believe a bad situation can be turned around. When something bad happens, optimists go into action to figure out what happened and what they can do to change or fix things. They take ownership for solving the problem because they feel they have control.

The optimistic thinker and the pessimistic thinker will evaluate and explain the same event differently, based on their individual and different interpretations of time, scope, and cause and their different perceptions of control and ownership. Their explanations determine how they feel about the situation and what courses of action they will take.

Explaining Bad Things That Happen

Let's look at how optimistic thinkers and pessimistic thinkers explain and interpret the situation when something bad happens.

The Optimistic View When Bad Things Happen

Optimistic thinkers see the time and scope of a bad situation as limited and the causes due to several factors. When something bad happens, they look for ways they can fix it or turn it around. They take ownership for changing or fixing a bad situation.

How Long Will This Thing Last?

When something bad happens, optimistic people see the situation as temporary. To them, a setback or problem is a one-time occurrence. They say things like, "This, too, will pass," "Things will be better tomorrow," and "It'll be better the next time." They are confident that other opportunities will arise and they will be able to try again.

Mark is a fund-raiser for a nonprofit organization. He set a goal to call thirty potential contributors every week. As you might expect, the majority of people reached through cold calling said no to his request for contributions, and Mark figured he had to make approximately twenty calls until he finally reached someone who would contribute. For every twenty calls, nineteen people would say no; one would say yes. "Each no brings me closer to a yes. I gotta keep calling to get to the next yes!" He even made a game of cold calling, referring to it as "Dialing for Dollars."

This way of viewing the situation is also used by successful salespeople, telemarketers, and collectors. They treat each "no" as a single occurrence and are confident that the next call will be a successful one.

How Far Does This Thing Reach?

Optimistic thinkers limit the scope, or extent, of a bad situation. When something bad happens, they see it as an isolated situation. An optimist would say, "Maybe my job is the pits right now, but at least the people I work with are great," or "I'm not happy about losing my window cubicle, but everything else at work is fine." Even if several bad things happen at once at work, optimistic thinkers separate the bad things from the good things. Some optimistic thinkers speak of compartmentalizing bad events so that one bad thing doesn't undermine their efforts in other job areas.

This ability to contain the problem helps optimists continue to function successfully, even happily, in the face of problems. They don't let problems in one area affect their efforts in other areas. By limiting the extent of the problem, optimistic thinkers figure out what specific steps they must take to fix things. An optimistic thinker might say, "That speech really bombed, but I got some good ideas about how to improve it for the next time." The optimistic customer service representative might think, "That customer was pretty angry that the billing got screwed up, but she didn't cancel the account. I think I know how to fix the billing problem and make sure it doesn't happen again."

Optimistic thinkers often regard a bad outcome as a challenge to keep plugging away. Thomas Edison invented the light bulb by experimenting. He discovered dozens of ways *not* to make a light bulb. The scientists who cloned sheep cells to create Dolly, the first cloned mammal, had dozens of failed attempts before they found success. Scientists and inventors simply cannot be pessimists; if they were, they would all quit after one or two failures.

Why Did This Happen?

To explain why something bad happened, optimistic thinkers look through an objective lens. They recognize and review all the forces that played a part in causing the bad event or situation. They identify what external factors contributed to the outcome and what part, if any, they themselves played. An optimistic-thinking entrepreneur might cite several reasons why her shop had a bad year—the store was located off the main shopping street; the economy was experiencing a downswing; a leaky roof ruined thousands of dollars worth of merchandise; she didn't target her advertising to the right audience.

When optimists identify how they themselves may have created or contributed to a problem, they don't beat themselves up. For instance, an optimist would say, "I forgot to do . . ." instead of "I failed to do . . . ." They don't internalize the bad thing, and they don't engage in excessive self-blame and self-recrimination.

Control and Ownership for Optimists

By looking for external factors that contributed to a bad situation, such as the shop owner's list above, optimists are not seeking to blame others for bad outcomes, nor are they using external factors to excuse their own shortcomings. Instead, they are trying to ascertain what, if anything, they can do to turn the situation around. Optimistic thinkers are confident that bad situations can be fixed. As they look over all the factors that contributed to failure, optimists identify the areas where they believe they have control—where they believe they can orchestrate a turnaround. They also identify the areas they cannot control or change.

When optimists feel they have control over a part of the problem, they take ownership for fixing it. If they believe they can fix it, they'll try. Even if the external circumstances are beyond an individual's control, optimistic thinkers still perceive they have *some* control, such as control over their response to the circumstances. They then take ownership for their responses.

For example, one morning I woke up and thought I'd suffered a stroke. One side of my face was paralyzed. I'd lost control of the facial muscles on that side. My face was contorted and my eyelid drooped. I looked in the mirror and saw a gargoyle.

It turns out I had a viral infection called Bell's Palsy, and I was scheduled to give a training session about dealing with change. I had no control over the disease or my facial muscles that week, but as an optimist, I believed I had control over how I felt about myself and how I would handle the training session. I thought, "I'll use my funny face to show that while you don't always have control over change, you do have control over your reactions to it."

I made the best of this situation. I explained to the group why I looked the way I did and asked them to focus with me on the course content. My humor and upbeat attitude got me through. My face and attitude turned out to be a powerful metaphor for the class participants and, according to their evaluation sheets, was an inspiration for many of them.

The Pessimistic View When Bad Things Happen

Pessimistic thinkers expand the time and scope of a bad situation beyond the immediate situation, and they believe they are to blame for its occurrence. When something bad happens, they feel helpless to change or fix it.

HOW LONG WILL THIS LAST?

Pessimistic people believe that problems or misfortunes will persist, and may even become permanent. They find it hard to bounce back from a setback because they have little hope that things will improve any time soon, if ever. They say things such as, "It's all over now," "This is a disaster; things will never be the same," and "I tried it once and it didn't work, so why should I try again?"

Among a group of corporate sales people, the pessimistic thinkers found cold calling extremely stressful. One such sales person found it very difficult to continue to make cold calls after receiving eight "no" responses in a row. He believed he had gotten on a bad streak that could last a long time.

How Far Does This Bad Thing Reach?

Pessimists don't limit the scope of a bad situation or event. To them, one bad event affects their whole job, even their whole life. They believe that ink from an overturned bottle will spread over everything on the desk—maybe even over everything in the office—and ruin all their work, their clothes, and the furniture. They let the effects of the bad situation seep into other parts of their jobs and lives. A pessimist might say things like this:

- "This is terrible; everything is falling apart."
- "I didn't get the promotion, so now I won't get a raise, which means we can't take that Hawaiian vacation this year, and my family will be disappointed and hate me."
- "I forgot to bring the extra slides. This will be the lamest presentation in company history. I'm doomed!"

Pessimists are the ones who have bad hair days. While they may crack jokes about their fate, they believe that the whole day is ruined if they can't get their hair to look good in the morning. Matt, a computer programmer, epitomized this way of thinking. A colleague stopped by his desk first thing in the morning and said, "How are you doing, guy?"

"This day is ruined."

"It's not even 8:30. What's wrong?"

Matt shook his head in disgust. "I just had a call from a very unhappy client. I hate it when days start like this. That bad taste in my mouth lasts all day." True to form, Matt, like other pessimistic thinkers, let one bad event affect everything else on the job that whole day, and he wasn't much fun at home that night, either.

When pessimistic thinkers believe that one bad thing sets off a chain of bad events, they're indulging in catastrophic thinking. This kind of thinking gives rise to feelings of tremendous worry. It can also create hopelessness in pessimists who believe that bad situations have enormous power reaching into all parts of their lives. Catastrophic thinking exaggerates; calling a problem a disaster, tragedy, or catastrophe increases the agony of the problem, along with the pessimist's anxiety.

Gena was a nurse educator in a large medical center. At the end of each class, she collected the evaluation sheets on which class participants would rate the effectiveness and value of the course, the handouts, and the trainer. Most of the time, Gena received the top ratings of nine or ten, which meant excellent. Occasionally, someone would rate her effectiveness as five or six, which meant average. She usually felt depressed for a couple of days when this happened. Once, she had a rating of one, very poor. Gena went into a tailspin. For days, all she could think about was the level-one rating. She began to question her competency as a trainer. She beat herself up over one poor rating out of the dozens of excellent ratings she had received. It's a pessimist's tendency to focus on one bad thing and to overlook, or even forget, the many good things that outweigh it.

Why Did This Happen?

When something bad happens, pessimistic thinkers blame themselves. They say things like this:
- "I should have known better."
- "I don't know what I'm doing."
- "I'm not good at these things."

Pessimistic thinkers believe bad things happen due to their own personal inadequacy or personal flaw. By taking responsibility for creating the bad situation, pessimists find it difficult to detach and look beyond themselves to consider external factors that may have contributed to the problem. The optimist can separate himself from a failure; the pessimist internalizes the failure. He becomes the failure.

Pessimists don't objectively look at what specific thing they did that may have created the bad situation. Instead, they personalize the problem. A pessimist won't simply say, "I miscalculated the cost estimate." Instead she says, "I'm terrible with numbers; I always mess up estimates; I'm such an idiot." While an optimist might say, "I miscalculated; I'll redo the numbers," the pessimist heaps herself with blame and makes a sweeping statement about her past, present, and future competency with numbers.

The pessimistic thinker may even extend the self-blame to situations beyond his or her control. For example, Gena, the nurse educator, had a group of attentive participants in one training session, but she focused on the one person who wasn't paying attention. She blamed herself for that one person's inattention. "If I were a better trainer, that man would be listening," she thought. Gena did not consider the possibility that an inattentive person might be distracted with personal or work problems. Gena inappropriately took responsibility for a situation over which she had no control.

CONTROL AND OWNERSHIP FOR PESSIMISTS

Pessimists own the problem and blame themselves, yet they also believe they have no control over its solution. They believe there's nothing they can do to fix or change things and may be convinced that doing anything else will make things worse, not better. In addition, pessimists become paralyzed by the huge scope of their problems, overwhelmed by the anxiety and the helplessness they feel. The paralysis keeps them from taking positive corrective action.

Not surprisingly, pessimists suffer depression more than optimists. Their thoughts that everything is awful (scope), it will be awful for eons (time), and it is all my fault (cause) are a perfect script for depression.

Explaining Good Things That Happen

As we've seen, optimists and pessimists explain the bad things that happen differently. They also differ in how they explain the good things that happen.

The Optimistic View When Good Things Happen

Optimistic thinkers expand the time and scope of a good situation and credit themselves for positive outcomes.

HOW LONG WILL THIS GOOD THING LAST?

When something good happens, optimists think it will continue, or may even become permanent. They believe good events aren't temporary, but are ongoing. One good thing gives rise to another good thing. They say things like, "I'm on a roll now," or "Everything's cooking; nothing can stop us now." For the optimist, the cookie jar keeps filling as one good thing begets another.

Kelly began working at a large insurance company as a customer service representative. Although she enjoyed her work, she decided after a few years that she wanted to do something else. The first time we had a coaching session, I was impressed with her optimistic visions for success. She investigated her career options and decided that public relations was a good match for her talents and interests. She started a certificate program at a university extension center to prepare herself. While doing this, she was promoted at work to assistant supervisor. Kelly optimistically took this as a sign that her company saw her potential and that she'd eventually find her dream job within the company. She also viewed the positive comments from her instructors as confirmations that she'd made a good career choice and would be a rousing success.

When she had completed the extension program, she met with the vice president of public relations for her company to get advice about finding her dream job. He told her bluntly that she would have difficulty finding such a job because her work experience did not match the requirements for a public relations position. Undaunted, Kelly made appointments to meet with PR managers at four companies. The first manager she interviewed complimented her on her enthusiasm, offered career advice, and encouraged her to go after what she wanted. After the meeting, Kelly thought, "I think it's all going to work out perfectly for me." Believing that one good experience can be multiplied, Kelly was confident that the other three managers would respond positively as well. Indeed, they did respond favorably, with one manager inviting her to apply for a position as a public relations assistant. A month after starting her search, Kelly had landed her dream job. She was not only optimistic, but also persistent in the face of obstacles. She had a can-do attitude.

How Far Does This Good Thing Reach?

For optimists, one good event has a positive impact on other parts of their jobs and lives. They think expansively: if something good happens on one project, something good will happen on other projects. They'll think things such as "Everything's great!" or "That turned out well, and I'm sure everything else will be fine, too," or "Everything's coming up roses!"

Reggie sold training videos to corporations. He worked for six months with a large, multi-state company, hoping eventually to make a sale. The day the contract was signed, Reggie felt he owned the planet. Back in the office, he announced, "I just landed paradise. The world is my candy store!" The brightness of his success with a customer he'd pursued for months infused everything in his life with a sweet, warm glow.

Why Did This Happen?

Optimistic thinkers believe that good things happen due to their own efforts. They have confidence in their abilities and credit themselves for the part they played in creating success, enlarging their impact on good outcomes. Optimistic thinkers say things like, "I'm really good at this," or "My hard work paid off," or "I knew exactly what to do, and it worked."

By feeling they are in control and have played a large part in creating a success, optimists believe they can repeat their successes. One success can motivate them to go after another. An optimist thinks, "If I did it once, I can do it again."

The Pessimistic View When Good Things Happen

Pessimistic thinkers narrow, or limit, the time and scope of a good situation. They look for external factors to explain positive outcomes and successes.

How Long Will This Good Thing Last?

Pessimistic thinkers believe that good news is temporary. They think good events or outcomes are random occurrences that will end soon. They say things such as, "I got a lucky break this time," or "This is too good to last," or "Enjoy our client's happiness now—they'll be complaining soon."

Gerald, who owned and managed a small printing business, had several good things happen one month. He acquired two lucrative contracts through referrals, he hired a new typesetter who proved to be a superior worker, and his business manager negotiated a great price for a new press. Rather than celebrating his good fortune, Gerald told his new assistant, "Things have been looking pretty good this month. I'm worried that something bad is going to happen. Somebody is going to screw up somewhere."

"That's not necessarily true," his optimistic assistant said. "Next month could be even better."

"It never happens that way. When too many good things happen, something bad comes along to balance things out. That's the way the world works."

Gerald, like most pessimists, engages in scarcity thinking. To him, good things are a limited resource. If several good things happen at one time, you're depleting the supply. Scarcity thinking feeds into his belief that you can't have good things for too long; you must pay for them with a bad thing. A pessimist sees copious good as an accumulation of debt—"I'll have to pay big-time for this windfall."

The pessimist sees the world as a big lending library where good things are available for a limited time in limited numbers, and he is competing with everyone else searching the shelves. The optimist sees the world as a huge virtual bookstore where many good things are available for as long as he wants them.

How Far Does This Good Thing Reach?

To pessimistic thinkers, the positive impact of a good event relates only to that event. While good things may be happening in their jobs, it doesn't affect the rest of a pessimist's life in a positive way as well. The goodness is contained in a bell jar. Similarly, they believe that they cannot repeat success in other situations. The pessimistic movie producer whose film has a great opening week box-office may think something like, "It was a fluke."

WHY DID THIS HAPPEN?

Pessimists rarely take credit for their successes. Instead, they point to external things or other people to explain their success. Pessimists think things such as, "I just got lucky," or "I was in the right place at the right time," or "I didn't really do anything; they did all the work," or "I couldn't have done it without Kevin's help." While it's important to acknowledge the contribution of others, particularly on team projects, pessimists go to extremes to denigrate their own contributions.

Fear of success is wrapped up in shrouds of pessimism. Believing they did nothing to create their own success, pessimists believe their victory is shallow, and they will soon crash and burn. In this way, pessimists become afraid of encountering success because they automatically fear they will be expected to repeat it.

When her senior colleague, Edward, suddenly took ill, Sherry, a junior auditor, was asked to fill in and give a presentation to management. Despite her nervousness and lack of speaking experience, Sherry successfully delivered the presentation to warm applause. Pleased, her manager told her afterwards, "You were great. I want you to deliver the management presentation next quarter."

Sherry panicked. "No, no, Edward made it easy for me with his notes and slides. Thank goodness no one asked me any really hard questions!"

Sherry was unable to give herself credit for how her own efforts had made for a successful presentation. She discounted the hours she put in the night before rehearsing and reviewing the notes and slides. She was convinced her success was due to a benevolent audience and her colleague's great work. She did not believe she could do it by herself.

Had Sherry been an optimistic thinker, she might have said, "It's a good thing I stayed up late to rehearse. I also took my time answering the questions so I wouldn't blurt out something wrong. And it helped that I arrived a little early so I could familiarize myself with the meeting room before the managers came it." An optimistic Sherry would have recognized specific things she did to contribute to her success; she would be confident she could repeat it.

What Kind of Thinker Are You?

As you read about optimistic and pessimistic thinking, you probably identified with one of the ways of thinking and explaining things. This exercise will get you thinking about your habitual way of explaining and responding to the things that happen in your life.

- What is your way of explaining things? When good things happen,
  do you tend to be optimistic or pessimistic? When bad things
  happen, do you tend to be optimistic or pessimistic?

- Think about your parents. When good things happened when you
  were a child, did your parents have an optimistic or pessimistic
  response? When bad things happened, did they have an optimistic or
  pessimistic response?

- Did you adopt your parents' way of thinking, or did you develop the
  opposite way of thinking? Why do you think you did that?

- How has your optimistic or pessimistic way of thinking helped or
  hindered you?

Similar Thought Process

Curiously, both optimists and pessimists use similar thinking patterns. Both can see a situation or event as temporary or permanent. Both can limit a situation or event to one aspect of their lives or expand it to reach into their whole lives. Both can see themselves, others, or outside forces as causing a situation or event. The tables on the opposite page summarize how optimists and pessimists respond to situations.

The difference is in how optimists and pessimists apply these ways of thinking to different situations.

Optimistic thinkers believe:
- The good things that happen to me will continue to happen.
- One good thing can have a positive impact on many other things in my life.
- I did something to make the good thing happen.

Pessimistic thinkers use this same line of thinking when they view bad things that happen to them. They believe:
- The bad things that happen to me will continue to happen.
- One bad thing can have a negative impact on many other things in my life.
- I did something to make the bad thing happen.

The presence or absence of hope in one's belief system determines whether optimism or pessimism prevails. Optimists may be demoralized by a horrible situation, but because they're filled with hope, they can put the situation into a manageable perspective. Hope gives them the resilience to bounce back from adversity.

Pessimists are weighted down by anchors of hopelessness. They view bad situations as all-encompassing and permanent, and they are often overcome by visions of helplessness as well. The combined punch of hopelessness and helplessness enervates them in the face of adversity.

Impact of Pessimistic and Optimistic Thinking on the Job

Optimistic thinking is a key ingredient to success in the workplace. We have seen in previous chapters how our thoughts give rise to our feelings and behaviors. Pessimistic thinking keeps us stuck in narrow, limiting behaviors that lead to frustration and discontent on the job. Optimistic thinking is the springboard to actions that lead to success.

How Optimists and Pessimists Explain Good and Bad Situations

When Something Bad Happens

	THE OPTIMISTIC VIEW	THE PESSIMISTIC VIEW
Time	Limits: Situation is temporary. "This won't last."	Expands: Situation is permanent or will continue. "This will go on forever."
Scope	Limits: Just one thing is bad. "It's just this thing; everything else is okay."	Expands: Everything is ruined. "One bad thing leads to another."
Cause	Externalizes: Looks for all the factors that contributed. "Let's see why this happened."	Internalizes: Blames self. "It's all my fault."
Ownership	Owns the solution: Takes responsibility for fixing the problem or changing own reaction. "Let's see what can be done."	Owns the problem: Feels paralyzed. "There is nothing I can do."

When Something Good Happens

	THE OPTIMISTIC VIEW	THE PESSIMISTIC VIEW
Time	Expands: Situation is permanent or will continue. "Everything's going to be great."	Limits: Situation is temporary. "This won't last."
Scope	Expands: Everything will go well. "One good thing leads to another."	Limits: Just this thing is good. "Yes, but . . . ."
Cause	Internalizes: I did something to make it happen. "I did it."	Externalizes: Outside forces made it happen; I played no part. "I just got lucky."
Ownership	Owns the success: "I know what I am doing."	Attributes success to others: "It just happened."

In chapter two I said that optimistic thinking ties directly to the key competencies that companies want in employees today. Optimism aligns with many of the new beliefs needed for success in the workplace.

When problems arise in the workplace, optimistic thinkers go into action: *What happened? Why? How can I fix it?* Their entrepreneurial approach to problems stems from their belief that they can dig in and control a manageable situation. They expect that things will turn out well, so they persist. They are willing to take risks. A risk that results in a successful outcome motivates optimists to take future risks; a risk resulting in a negative outcome becomes an opportunity to learn and to try again.

Pessimistic thinkers are less effective at solving difficult problems because they are more likely to become paralyzed or overwhelmed. They feel they have no control; they don't believe they can solve anything. While optimists own the solution to the problem, pessimists own the problem. Pessimists focus inwardly on how they created the problem, rather than looking objectively at the bigger picture to create resolutions.

Expecting the worst, pessimists give up easily when they encounter difficulties. They do not bounce back from problems quickly. They are reluctant to take risks because they focus on thoughts of failure instead of thoughts of success; they take failure as a statement of their competence. If they take a risk and succeed, they do not feel encouraged. They believe that success is a random event, like pulling the arm of a winning slot machine— it is unlikely to occur again, and besides, the winnings are taxable!

Optimists respond quickly to problems. At the first sign of an impending break in the levee, they start sand-bagging before the situation gets out of hand. Pessimists compound problems with self-defeating thoughts. "The levee will break and flood the whole town. I'll never shore up the weak spot—why bother to try?"

In stressful situations, optimists take action. They look for changes they can make to reduce or eliminate the source of stress. Those changes may be in themselves, too. Pessimists are more passive under stress. They are more likely to brood, complain, or gossip. Another pessimistic coping response is to try to forget the whole thing. For example, they may fantasize about being saved by a winning lottery pick.

Optimists approach change with the belief that everything will turn out fine. Optimists see change as a challenge and a growth opportunity. Even when change is at first unwelcome, they find ways to embrace change in the midst of the uncertainty and confusion. Optimists are not defeated by the problems that naturally arise when serious change occurs.

Pessimists subscribe to Murphy's Law—whatever can go wrong will go wrong. Some pessimists defend their thinking by claiming they are being realistic—"I'm not being pessimistic; I'm just being realistic." However, there is a big difference between pervasive pessimism and what we might call healthy pessimism. Healthy pessimism starts with the pessimist's assumption that if something can go wrong, it will. Then it switches to the optimist's view that problems can be solved. A healthy pessimist lists all the bad things that could happen, then shifts to creative problem solving to develop realistic options and strategies to handle the difficulties that may arise. Healthy pessimism is an appropriate approach to assessing risky situations or determining weaknesses in a proposal under consideration. It is valuable to people responsible for financial reporting in an organization where optimism must be tempered with a realistic assessment of the financial data. This is still quite different from the pervasive pessimist who simply lists all the bad things that will happen and then withdraws.

For example, the slashing of the city budget forced the social services department to lay off two social workers, which increased the work load for the four remaining social workers. No one was happy with that, and the two pessimistic thinkers in the group promptly complained. They took the cutbacks personally, internalizing the stress of their increased workload. They did not employ healthy pessimism; theirs was pervasive. The two optimists responded by changing their approach to handling their cases. Their creative juices started flowing, and they devised new programs that were less costly to administer and better served their clients.

It has been said that success is ten percent inspiration and ninety percent perspiration. Optimistic thinkers persist because they believe they'll ultimately succeed. They own and enjoy their successes, and one success motivates them to create another. They are both independent and entrepreneurial.

Pessimists don't see a link between their actions and success; they don't believe they can repeat a win. On the job, this lack of confidence makes them dependent on other people or outside factors to motivate them. As we saw for Gerald, the print shop owner, some pessimists believe they'll have to pay for their success. The result can be that a pessimist who succeeds in one area of the job suddenly has problems in another area.

Optimists generally relate better to their co-workers because most people are more attracted to positive people than to negative people. Optimists can rally others to action, while pessimists can discourage action. Listen to the speeches of political, military, and spiritual leaders. Hear how they capture people's attention, votes, and hearts. Even prophets of doom who warn the end of the world is near (quite a pessimistic thought) convince people to follow behind them by painting an optimistic new worldview of the paradise that awaits believers.

Co-workers often view pessimists as wet blankets who put a damper on other people's happiness or feelings of success. Pessimists' comments can be demoralizing to others in a group setting.

When restructuring for a metropolitan medical center led to dozens of layoffs, a disgruntled staff—from nurses to x-ray technicians—complained loudly and bitterly about how the cutbacks threatened the quality of care in the hospital. They did not consider the impact of their gloomy predictions on their patients, and many patients became distressed when they heard the pessimistic comments. Ironically, the staff and caregivers were so concerned about the quality of care in the facility that they did not think about the toxicity of their pessimistic behavior and complaints on their patients.

You Find What You Seek

You may have heard the tale of a medieval gatekeeper who guarded the entrance to a small village. One day a man rode up on a horse and said to the gatekeeper, "I'm seeking a new place to live. Everywhere I go, I find villages filled with terrible people. They gossip and say hurtful things about each other. They steal from one another. They turn their backs on someone in need. Tell me, what are the people like here?"

The gatekeeper said to the man, "I'll save you time. You had better move on because the people in this village are just as you described."

The next day, another rider appeared and approached the gatekeeper. He said, "I'm looking for a new place to live, for my own village has become too crowded. The other villages I have visited so far are filled with wonderful people. They are respectful of each other. They share their bounty. They care about each other and help others in need. Tell me, how are the people here?"

The gatekeeper opened the gates to the village. "Welcome," he said. "The people in this village are just as you described."

The lesson is that we find what we seek. We look for evidence to support our beliefs and assumptions. The first man looked for terrible, hurtful people, and he found them everywhere he looked. The second man looked for caring, respectful people, and he found them everywhere he looked.

You can apply this fable to your own life by asking yourself, "What do I seek? Through which lens—pessimism or optimism—am I looking?"

Rhonda and Martin Find What They Seek

For Rhonda and Martin, the announcement of the department closure came two days before the company's annual picnic. When a co-worker later asked them if they were attending the picnic, Rhonda said, "Why should I bother? I don't feel like I'm a part of this company anymore." Martin said, "Sure, I'm going. This could be my last chance to see all the great people I've worked with for so long."

RHONDA'S RESPONSE

After some goading by her co-workers, Rhonda decided she'd attend the picnic after all. Yet at the picnic, her face revealed a woman in pain, prompting several to inquire if she were okay. She responded, "I haven't been feeling very good since I found out they're laying me off after twenty years of loyalty."

Her mournful tone elicited comments of sympathy. One person said, "I'm sure you'll find something in no time."

"Yeah, maybe," Rhonda sighed deeply. "But I heard the market's lousy and I'm over forty! A friend of mine looked for four months before she found anything." Another person said, "At least you're getting a good severance package. You can pay the bills while you look."

"I guess it's better than nothing," Rhonda shrugged. "I just hope I don't have an accident or get really sick and have to use all the money for doctor's bills."

Her friends exchanged glances with each other, then one said, "Well, we better go. The water balloon race is about to start."

As her friends walked away, Rhonda glanced around the picnic grounds to locate the food kiosks. She decided she'd just get something to eat and then go home. "It was a big, big mistake to come," she thought. "Sure, those people can be upbeat—they still have jobs! I knew I'd feel lousy all day. I should have stayed in bed."

MARTIN'S RESPONSE

Martin awoke on the morning of the picnic feeling sad that he would be losing his job. He considered skipping the picnic, but he decided to put aside the sad feelings for the day and enjoy being with friends. Once there, he ran into several people he hadn't seen for awhile. They asked him how things were going, and he said, "Well, in general, fine. Unfortunately, I just found out that my job is being terminated at the end of the month, so it looks as if it's time to polish up the old résumé. If you have any suggestions or leads, let me know."

"Call me next week," someone said. "I might know of an opening for you." Another person gave him the name of a good recruiter, and a third person offered to look over his résumé and give him ideas for revamping it.

The offers of help excited Martin, and he thought, "I'm glad I asked them for help. I have great friends to support me." By the time Martin left the picnic at sunset, he had gotten more leads and had exchanged telephone numbers with several people who wanted to take him to lunch. He headed home tired, but eager to start his job search.

Rhonda did not have a good time at the picnic and blamed herself for letting others talk her into going. The pain of the job loss affected her facial expression, her behavior, and her entire day. She responded to suggestions with a "Yes, but . . . ." This put people off, and they didn't hang around to offer any more help or to exchange telephone numbers.

Martin kept his feelings of sadness limited to the job loss. He was able to enjoy himself at the picnic. He put a positive spin on his situation, and encouraged others to share ideas with him. He left the picnic feeling motivated and helpful.

Rhonda may have thought, "Once you get laid off, you become a nobody. No one wants anything to do with you." She couldn't see that her pessimistic thinking and negativity drove them away. She left the picnic feeling miserable.

Most people want to help others in need. Since networking is one of the most successful techniques for finding a job, any job seeker should take advantage of the advice and assistance others willingly provide. Martin had no trouble eliciting useful suggestions from people when they heard about his situation. His upbeat attitude attracted people, and his positive response to their suggestions encouraged them to support him.

Rhonda and Martin's experiences illustrate the concept of the self-fulfilling prophecy, which is when your belief becomes your reality, and prophecies become self-fulfilling because of what you think, feel, and do. You may recall Eric, from chapter three, who felt isolated from his co-workers and longed to feel part of the group. He thought pessimistically, "I don't get along easily with people; I'm a loner." Believing he couldn't get along with others, he didn't try. He didn't do the things that more sociable people do. He didn't say hello to people, join in the casual morning conversation in the coffee room, or invite a co-worker to go to lunch. By acting in a way consistent with his pessimistic view of himself as a loner, he fulfilled his prophecy.

What's Your Habit?

You are capable of both optimistic and pessimistic thinking. Influences during childhood led you to choose one predominant way of explaining events, and that particular style became your habit, the theme of your scripts.

Perhaps you have discovered you developed the habit of pessimistic thinking because it was the predominant style of thinking in your family. Leonard, for example, identified himself as a pessimist. "My mother was seriously ill for months with pneumonia, and we were worried that she might not survive. Fortunately, she recovered and went back to her job. After about two weeks, she came home from work one day really upset. She told my dad that she was hurt that the people at work welcomed her back, but no one asked her how she was, and nobody seemed interested in hearing the details of her illness. She couldn't celebrate the good news about her own health; she could only complain about how others acted. I realized as I recalled this scene that, just like her, I collect all the bad feelings I have instead of keeping my eye on my successes."

Your style of thinking has molded your basic beliefs about yourself and the world. Negative beliefs are grounded in pessimism. To rewrite your scripts, you need to replace unhealthy pessimism with healthy optimism.

Change to the Lens of Optimism

Just as a cinematographer chooses a lens through which to shoot a movie scene, you can choose a lens of pessimism or optimism. Looking through the optimistic lens changes your thinking; and when you change your thinking, you change your feelings about yourself and your situation. Optimistic thinking is successful thinking.

Pessimists sometimes say, "I don't know how to think like an optimist." Yet, it's not *how* that needs to change; it's *when*. As we've seen, pessimistic thinkers already know how to contain or limit the impact of an event, and they know how to expand the impact of an event. To think optimistically, the pessimist needs to relearn when to contain the event and when to expand it.

If you are a pessimistic thinker, you need to take your way of explaining and interpreting negative situations and apply it to positive situations. You need to take your way of explaining and interpreting positive situations and apply it to negative situations. By swapping your ways of interpreting and explaining good and bad events, you use successful thinking patterns to change your old way of responding to life situations.

Babies Are Optimists

Even the staunchest pessimists were born with the seeds of optimism. Think about babies leaning to walk. They pull or push themselves up, take a tentative step, stumble, and fall down. Then they start all over again. They go through this process hundreds of times, seemingly never discouraged by their failure to walk. All of us were babies once, and we all learned to walk from each unsuccessful attempt. We kept improving. Each attempt brought us closer to our goal.

Stephen, an entrepreneur, had several businesses go belly up. As he was about to embark on a new venture, a friend asked him how he could believe in his newest business when the others had been failures. "They weren't failures; they were learning experiences," Stephen said. "I know what I did wrong those other times, so I won't repeat those mistakes this time." That was six years ago. Now his business has tripled its revenue and is about to expand into other states. Stephen never considered himself a failure; he considered himself a student who viewed each business opportunity as a training ground for his eventual success.

Successful entrepreneurs also separate something that didn't work from themselves as people. "The business failed, but that doesn't mean *I'm* a failure."

Dispute the Pessimistic View

When you assume the director's role for *My Successful Career*, you view your history and your current situation through an objective lens. You've learned to use objectivity to challenge your old scripts. Use that same process to challenge your unsuccessful, pessimistic thoughts. When you challenge something, you use an intellectual process, not an emotional one. The intellectual process helps you trade your pessimistic thinking for successful, optimistic thinking.

Pessimists believe they have great power when something goes wrong, but no power when something goes right. This is irrational thinking. How can you be powerful only when things are negative, yet powerless when things

Dispute the Pessimistic View

Return to the situation you identified in chapter four in exercise 4-A on page 94 or think of another uncomfortable situation at work. Take a fresh look at the situation through an objective lens and ask yourself the following questions:

- What do you believe about yourself in this situation? Is this optimistic or pessimistic thinking?

- How has your pessimistic thinking contributed to how you feel about this situation? How do you feel about yourself in this situation?

- What do you want to believe about yourself in this situation? Make a list of what you want to believe—e.g., I'm capable, competent, intelligent, reliable, trustworthy, responsible.

- What in this situation do you have control over? What things can you change to improve or fix it?

- If the external circumstances are beyond your control, what can you change in your thinking? For example, say you're having problems dealing with your company's rapid reorganizing. You have no control over the fact that changes are occurring. However, you *do* have control over your reactions to the changes. You can choose to have an optimistic reaction.

are successful? This kind of thinking can be traced back to one's basic beliefs: if you believe, "I'm not okay, I'm a bad person," then it follows that you believe you only have the power to make bad things happen.

When good and bad things happen to you, you want to continue to look through the lens of optimism. When pessimistic thoughts arise, the director has to step in and say "Cut!" Your pessimistic thinking keeps you stuck playing the role of the helpless, hopeless character. Replace the pessimistic thoughts with optimistic thoughts.

When you start to think this . . .	*Replace it with this . . .*
• It'll never work.	• It could work. Let's try it and see.
• Everything is ruined.	• Here are all the things that are okay. (List them on a piece of paper.)
• This is going to be a terrible day.	• I can turn this day around.
• This day was a disaster.	• Tomorrow will be better.
• I'm a failure.	• I'm having problems with this one thing. What can I do to resolve it?
• Yes, but . . . (litany of bad things)	• Yes, and . . . (list good things)
• Why bother. Nothing I do works.	• Let me give it a try.

What You Focus on Increases

You've probably had the experience of coming across a word you've never heard before—such as epiphany—on the news or in a magazine. Then you hear or read about someone's *epiphany* two days later, and someone else's *epiphany* a day after that. How could it be that suddenly everyone is using *epiphany*?

The word has always been there, but because you weren't paying attention to it, you missed it every time it crossed your path. Now that you're paying attention, you find the word everywhere.

Whatever we pay attention to increases. If you pay attention to negativity, self-blame, and self-misery, hideous things bombard your mind, keeping you miserable at work and limiting your success. By turning your attention to positives, successes, and rewards, your consciousness fills with much more fulfilling thoughts and perceptions.

As Rhonda and Martin pursue their job searches, Rhonda's pessimism and Martin's optimism play key roles in determining their future. Rhonda's pessimism, and her expectation that job hunting is filled with pain, causes her to focus on the misery she is experiencing. Each task in her job search—from writing a résumé to making calls to going on interviews—becomes an arduous process. She doesn't take advantage of the support of outplacement counseling provided by her company.

Rhonda is primed to become very discouraged if her first few leads turn into dead ends or her first few interviews don't yield job offers. She'll think something like, "It's true that nobody wants to hire someone who's been laid off." By focusing on this belief, which she thinks is supported by the empirical evidence of her failures, she may end up sabotaging herself in further interviews by coming across as passive, strained, and defeated. She may become so discouraged that she even stops looking for a while.

Martin's optimistic outlook turns his job search into an adventure—*My Wonderful Job Search*—rather than an endurance test. He approaches each job search activity as a step that brings him closer to his goal, and he maintains his belief, "I know there's something out there for me. I just have to keep looking." He looks at his age as a positive; he sees years of maturity, wisdom, and experience. If he does not get a job after several interviews, he'll review how the interviews went to see what he might do differently. He may also revise his résumé to target it for specific jobs, and, most important of all, he will keep looking and talking to people for leads. These are excellent strategies for successful job seeking. Job seekers who keep searching eventually find jobs; those who stop looking only find misery.

You get what you expect, and you will find what you look for. Focus on the positive things in your job, and they will appear. Continue to look for the positives, and they will increase.

Part Three

ACTION!

Put Your New Scripts and Behaviors to Work

Chapter 7

The Editing Room
Releasing Childhood Roles and Scripts

In the life of every Hollywood movie, cutting and revising is a natural part of the creative process. It happens with the script long before production begins, and it continues all the way through production and even into postproduction. Even after a movie has been released, many of its principal artists still replay it in their minds, cutting and revising for the fun of it, wondering how they could have done a scene differently.

You can do the same thing with your own production of *My Successful Career*. You can cut and revise the script you live and work by. You can cut and revise the production of your life. You can even work on your script in postproduction by looking back on your history and viewing it in a different context.

If you have read this far and done the exercises, you most likely see that the scripts you developed long ago and the role you have been playing since then don't produce success in today's modern, rapidly changing workplace. You probably see how revising your beliefs, thoughts, feelings, and behaviors can propel you closer to success.

Maybe you've tried to rewrite and update your old scripts, but . . . well, it just doesn't seem to be working. You understand intellectually what you are supposed to do, and you want to change; but you just can't seem to let go of that old stuff.

Making changes is not always easy. You have been playing a role for how long—twenty, thirty, forty, or more years? You are trying to take on a new role, and just as it takes an actor time to fully learn a new part, it is going to take you time to learn your new role and to play it well. Changes like these don't happen overnight.

Your scripts are familiar and comfortable for you. You can perform them without much thought. Thinking, feeling, and doing something new requires active thought and motivation. It also requires active attention. Much of the time, we live life as if we are on autopilot, just attending to our business and pleasure. Making changes requires bringing into our daily lives and actions a conscious level of awareness that we seldom have. Making changes also requires that we experience some discomfort until we become familiar with new scripts and new roles.

But there are deeper reasons why we cling to the old ways. We have an investment in staying the same. Our scripts don't exist in a void. They served a purpose for us when we developed them, and they continue to serve a purpose today. They helped us cope with the complexities of life and helped us get what we needed. We can't toss them aside like old running shoes until we've recognized and honored the purpose they served. The challenge is to figure out what that purpose was.

Decoding the Purpose

In spy movies, the hero has to decode the messages from the enemy to figure out what the enemy is really up to. Our scripts have secret messages locked within them, too, and we have to be heroic to decode them. When we crack the code, we will discover the purpose of our scripts and understand the underlying reasons why we continue to act out those scripts, even when they are outdated and unhealthy. This is why in chapter four I asked you to look at your family history. That is where the secrets are stashed, and that is where the coded messages were first written.

The coded messages are the deeper meanings to our scripts. Until we figure them out, we usually can't move on. Once we recognize and decode them, the purpose of our scripts is revealed. The real key to being able to switch to a new script is to understand why we wrote the old script in the first place.

It is not always easy to dig below the surface of our script to decode the underlying purpose for our beliefs and actions. Our deep emotional investment in our scripts keeps us from seeing the reality of our situation. It is as if we have a blind spot. Our minds defend, rationalize, and justify our current position. We usually minimize the impact of our old scripts and behaviors.

I've had clients tell me, "I don't do this so much, just sometimes," or "It is not such a big deal."

Perhaps another reason it is hard for us to identify the underlying purpose is we know, at some level, that once we find and acknowledge that purpose, there is no going back. Our script reveals our truth, and once we tell the truth, we can never be the same. That, of course, is what change is all about. It is about becoming a different person and exchanging the unhappiness for a new and better life.

Connections to the Past

Why would anyone continue to use old scripts with self-defeating behaviors? There are several reasons, often complex and interrelated. Just like a movie script, your own scripts have twists and turns, plots and subplots; and trying to figure out the purpose they serve is sometimes very challenging.

When you start to dig down, you begin to discover the reasons for your old scripts: they connect you to your past. Whether you are aware of it or not, your old scripts stir up old memories and emotions that provide your connection to the past. That is why scripts are so hard to give up: they provide a link that is important to you. If your past and your family history were pleasant, it is understandable that you would want to maintain a connection to it. But, even if your past was downright horrible, you still want a connection to it because your whole history is embodied in that past. You are the sum total of all the experiences you've had. Turning your back on your past denies some part of yourself. The connection to your history is so important to you that you may be willing to sabotage your success to maintain that connection.

To grow, your task is to choose and preserve parts from your past that work and change the parts that don't work. Sometimes it is tricky to look at the past and separate the parts that work from the parts that don't. Some people who endured a miserable childhood maintain a fantasy about what it was like, denying how bad it was. For example, children who grew up in a household where the parents fought constantly often believe that they were bad and that is why their parents fought. They maintain this image of themselves from a desperate desire to preserve a fantasy image of their parents as loving and nurturing. When they look back at their past through the eyes of the adult director, it disturbs them to see that their mother and father really were cruel to each other and unable to resolve problems in a more mature way.

You continue to use your old scripts for several reasons:

- To gain approval from your parents
- To maintain a connection with them
- To maintain ties with other family members
- To get attention and sympathy from others
- To preserve an image of yourself

We call these reasons hidden payoffs. They are *hidden* because what we get from them—the payoff or reward—is not immediately apparent.

For example, maybe you gobble down several cookies during a rough day at work. The instant gain may be to make you feel better by relieving your immediate anxiety and stress. Many people have favorite foods they like to eat to make them feel happy. If you delve deeper into your history and look at how chocolate cookies came to mean happiness, you might remember that your mother gave you sweet foods to comfort you and make you feel better when you felt stressed. The hidden payoff for eating the cookies as an adult is that it brings back distant memories of feeling loved and cared for by your mother. You may be vaguely aware of these memories on a conscious level; primarily you're aware that eating cookies makes you feel secure and comforted.

Will Your Success Hurt Someone?

Powerful underlying purposes exist for many self-defeating behaviors. One may be that you are afraid your success will hurt someone—your parents, siblings, spouse, children, or even your co-workers. Remember Tony, the sales rep, who fears his father will be hurt if he does better than Dad? You may fear that too much success might cause your parents or someone else to abandon you. You imagine that by being successful you somehow injure them. If you do achieve success, you may believe you must pay for your success. The price of success is often tremendous anxiety, guilt, or abandonment. Rather than suffer these painful circumstances, we choose to sabotage ourselves and thus ensure we don't hurt the people we care about. The irony, of course, is that in our attempt to avoid hurting others, we frequently hurt ourselves.

Of course, you are seldom aware of any of these reasons. They are usually out of the realm of your awareness and consciousness. However, they are powerful because they provide the crucial link to your past.

Underlying Purposes and Hidden Payoffs

Let's do some digging beneath several people's scripts to identify the underlying purposes and hidden payoffs that prevent them from enjoying success today.

Some cultures, such as Asian cultures, openly emphasize honoring one's family and heritage. In non-Asian cultures, children unconsciously honor their parents and cultures through their scripts. Both of Russell's parents were doctors, and he was expected to become a doctor, too. In his teens he played cello in a youth orchestra and dreamed of being a symphony musician, but that was not to be. To fulfill his parents' expectations, Russell dutifully went to medical school and opened his own practice, putting aside his musical aspirations.

To many, Russell today appears to be a great success. Yet all his adult life, he has suffered terrible anxiety attacks that have interfered with his work and many other aspects of his life. He is living out his parents' script—at a great personal cost. Even now, as he enters his forties, with his parents in their seventies, Russell feels that if he changes careers, or even reduces his medical practice so he could spend more time practicing his music, he will be disappointing his parents. Although he knows it is irrational, deep down he believes that pursuing his musical passions is being disloyal to his parents, a disloyalty that could hasten their death.

For some people, doing better than their parents and other family members in their careers is a type of disloyalty that could hurt the family. Patrick grew up in a large family and won scholarships to an Ivy League university, where he quickly completed his undergraduate degree and went on to earn his MBA. At graduation, he was recruited by a large investment brokerage firm and is considered one of its rising stars. Recently, he was tapped to head up the firm's overseas division. To most who know him, Patrick appears to be a rousing success. He has a high-profile job, earns a handsome salary, and has a wonderful wife and two bright, active children. Yet unbeknown to anyone, Patrick struggles at work. He knows that to increase the business, he has to make some aggressive moves to acquire the overseas division of another investment firm. But he does not feel very aggressive, and he wonders if he really wants this new job.

At the heart of Patrick's confusion and uncertainty is a strong feeling that he has been disloyal to his family; he's broken the unwritten rules about the work the men in his family do. His father struggled for years to support his large family on a bus driver's income. Patrick's brothers work in blue collar jobs, and his sister married a man in the construction business. Patrick was the first in his family to go to college, and the first to land a white collar job. He fears they say behind his back, "You're not one of us anymore."

He's also afraid that his success will hurt his family in some way. He has always downplayed his achievements to them, and now he hesitates to tell his brothers and sister about his recent promotion. "Oh, Mr. Big Shot," he imagines them saying. "Thinks he's so much better than we are." He imagines his older brother looking at his well-cut suits and saying, in a voice tinged with jealousy, "Look at my little brother, the broker, in his fancy suits."

He doesn't want to seem better than they are. Deep down he is afraid they'll abandon him because he's different. Patrick can't enjoy his success when he's with them. He may unconsciously limit his successes in the future so he won't break the unwritten blue collar family code.

The fear that your success will hurt your parents or other family members can show up in various ways. You may deliberately, yet unconsciously, hide your skills and abilities so as not to compete with anyone. As a child, Gabriella was prettier, smarter, and more talented than her sister, Shana. Everyone—aunts, uncles, neighbors, teachers—told her, directly or indirectly, that she was the star of the family. When she won a talent contest at the age of eight, her mother told her not to flaunt her achievement. She even put Gabriella's large trophy in a basement storeroom so that, as she put it, "Your sister won't be jealous." When neighbors stopped them on the street to offer congratulations for winning the contest, her mother pushed Gabriella's sister forward, saying, "Gabriella isn't the only talented one. Shana knows how to sing and dance, too."

Gabriella began to hold back so that she wouldn't outshine her sister. The more successful she felt, the more her anxiety and guilt increased that she might hurt her sister. Unconsciously, she wrote her script to limit herself, thus protecting her sister. To calm her anxiety, she starting eating more, taking seconds at dinner, and snacking on sweets. Her resulting weight-gain kept her fatter than her lithesome sister.

As an adult, she continued to confine her talents. She would not speak up to claim credit for her part in a team project because she didn't want to hurt any team member's feelings. When she was promoted, she worried that her co-workers would feel jealous, another unconscious connection to her sister.

Some people try to win their parents' attention by playing the part of the helpless victim. The hope that someone (especially your mother or father) will come to rescue you, to comfort you, and to keep the bullies and hurtful people away from you is a very appealing fantasy, but the fantasy gets written into our scripts and leads to self-defeating behavior. The behaviors can take the form of blaming others for your problems, whining and complaining about other people, and acting helpless. Given that many victims seem to be so miserable, what could be the hidden payoff for them? For many victims, suffering brings attention. Complaining with a co-worker about how you didn't get picked for a project team creates a feeling of closeness and the illusion that someone cares about how you feel.

For some people, the hidden payoff in their scripts is preserving a certain image they have of themselves, even if that image is that they are failures. For example, children raised by negative, highly critical parents may grow up thinking they are failures and disappointments to their parents, and that they can do nothing right. They develop scripts in which they play the failure, and in adult life they bring these scripts into the workplace.

Continuing to fail not only preserves their own image, but also maintains their connection to their family and their position in it. Unconsciously, they think, This is who I am—I'm the failure, the big disappointment. As painful as that role may be, it is familiar pain.

The Failure is not the only role people play in their families. Other roles are caretaker, negotiator, troublemaker, or rebel. Rebecca finds herself conflicted as she tries both to preserve a certain image of herself and to maintain her connection to her family. Rebecca was always the responsible one in her family. She took care of everyone. She protected her mother from the rages of her drunken father, and she raised her two younger sisters when her mother suffered a nervous breakdown. Today, she is the family breadwinner, supporting not only her own teenaged children, but also her mother, a divorced sister, and her sister's child. She has a responsible position supervising tellers in a bank, but she's worried that an upcoming merger with another bank may result in cutbacks and the elimination of her job.

Rebecca's manager told her a year ago that changes in the banking industry mean that jobs such as hers are either being phased out or are changing and will require more technical skills. He advised her then to start preparing for the changes by going back to school or looking for a different position. The open positions in the bank she is qualified for require a longer commute or weekend work. Going back to school would take up her evening hours.

Rebecca feels stuck. She is unhappy with the uncertainty of her current position, but when she thinks about working farther away or going back to school, her thoughts fly to her family. "They need me," she thinks. "I'm all they have. Their needs are more important than mine." She feels she can't start a job search or go back to school until her children are grown and gone and her sister has found a place of her own, too. Rebecca is so rattled that she has spun a whole disaster fantasy—she enrolls in night classes, her teenagers start hanging out on street corners, her mother has another nervous break-down, and her sister begins to drink as heavily as their father did. Rebecca believes that focusing on her own success will cause her to neglect her family, who will suffer greatly. Her hidden payoff is that she preserves her role of caretaker, thereby maintaining her family.

Like Rebecca, many women put other people's needs ahead of their own. To preserve their marriage, and to maintain their husband's status as senior wage earner, some women unconsciously sabotage themselves at work. Elvira and her husband, Javier, both work for the same company. Even though they work in different divisions—Elvira is a programmer and Javier is a data pro-cessing manager—many people in the company know they are married. Elvira consistently downplays her intelligence and her cleverness, yet her manager thinks Elvira should take on more complex projects. When he put Elvira in charge of a large project that gave her more visibility, she struggled to keep the project on track. Elvira explained her difficulties by saying she felt un-comfortable handling such a large project. However, the underlying reason was that she feared that her success in delivering a big project on time and on budget would threaten her husband. He regularly handled big, highly visible projects. Elvira didn't think there was room in her marriage for two success-ful project managers. Like Gabriella, who doesn't want her sister to suffer jeal-ousy, Elvira ensures her husband will never experience jealousy over her success.

People who have escaped death in a terrible accident that killed others—or horrendous circumstances such as a massacre, holocaust, or war—often experi-ence what is called survivor guilt. They feel guilty for having survived when others died. Survivor guilt is not limited to situations that involve death, however. People who have overcome oppressive circumstances, such as crushing poverty or abusive situations, can also experience survivor guilt. Although they escaped from miserable conditions and made a better life for themselves, they feel guilty about friends and family left behind. They question whether they deserve the better life they have created. Sometimes they can't enjoy their success; sometimes they sabotage it. For some, the guilt can become so great that they close the door on their past and break off all contact with their family.

Tara, a high school student in a small town, dreamed of going to college. Her English teacher encouraged her to apply for a scholarship to a large university in another state. When she won the scholarship, her brothers and some of her friends accused her of turning her back on them by accepting the scholarship. Tara handled the rigors of her freshman year in a large school in an unfamiliar place, but when she returned home for the summer, her brothers taunted her about speaking differently and claimed that her disinterest in spending time with her former friends proved she had changed. Midway through her sophomore year, she began to have problems at school, missing deadlines for papers, losing homework, and doing poorly on tests. She went home for the Christmas holidays and talked about her problems with her mother. Hating to see her daughter struggle, her mother counseled Tara to stay home and take a job in town. Tara, feeling the pull of her family connection, decided to take her mother's advice.

While some people engage in self-defeating behaviors to avoid being abandoned by their family, others sabotage themselves in their desires to become autonomous. They continue to fight a battle for independence long after they have left home, settled into their own homes, and established their own lives.

Adele's parents pushed her to go to college, beginning in ninth grade when she argued with her mother over what elective to take. She wanted to take choir because she loved to sing. Her mother insisted she take French because having several years of a foreign language would make her college applications more attractive. Adele took French for four years, was later accepted at the university, then dropped out after a couple of semesters. Now in her forties, she regrets having left school and suspects the lack of a degree has held her back in her career. Every time she contemplated returning to school, she found a reason not to do so—lack of money, lack of time due to a demanding job, and uncertainty about what to study. Now she's beginning to feel she is too old. But the underlying reason for dropping out of school and staying away all these years is that she is still trying to assert her independence from her parents. Unconsciously, she has been thinking if a university education is that important to them, she would show her independence by not getting one.

Tara chose to please her mother by complying with her mother's wishes. Adele chose *not* to please her mother by doing the opposite of what her mother wanted. In both cases, the women ended up limiting themselves by not going to college.

Describe Success

This exercise can help you decode your scripts and identify the underlying purpose for them.

In exercise 2-C in chapter two on page 52, you defined what success would look like for you. Review your description of success and then answer the following questions. You will probably find it helpful to write your answers on a piece of paper.

- What is the worst that could happen if you achieve success?

- How do your old scripts connect you to your parents or to other important people in your past who cared for you?

- What impact—positive or negative—will your success have on your:
  - —parents   —children
  - —siblings   —friends
  - —spouse   —co-workers

- Who do you believe will be hurt by your success? Who will be jealous? Who will you surpass if you are successful?

- Are these concerns real, or are they fantasies? What evidence do you have that these concerns are real? What evidence do you have that what you believe will come true?

- Who will gain and who will lose if you continue to use your old self-defeating scripts?

- Who will gain and who will lose if you make changes and start using new scripts?

Changing Feels Like Death

Your desires to reap the hidden payoffs—such as maintaining a connection with your parents and ensuring that no one suffers—are strong reasons for you to hang onto your old scripts. There's another reason, too, and this has to do with almost any change you are contemplating. Letting go of old scripts means you have to let go of something—even if it is letting go of something painful.

Letting go may also mean you have to let go of something about yourself. This can feel as if you are cutting out—even killing—parts of yourself. You can very deliberately go through the process of identifying the underlying purpose for your script, and then you may reach a point where you say, "Okay, I see why I created this script when I was young, and now it is holding me back. But if I don't continue to use this script, what will I do? Who am I if I don't play this role? What role will I play?"

Lily wanted to understand the underlying reasons for the depression that had been with her for as long as she could remember. She recognized her depression was a way to stay connected to her father, who had also suffered deep depressions since leaving China many years ago. She saw how her pessimistic thinking created her feelings of hopelessness and helplessness. When she realized she could change her thinking to successful, optimistic thinking, she felt relieved that she could make her depression go away.

Then, as she pondered more, she suddenly felt as if she were facing an incredible void. "Who am I if I'm not depressed about work?" she asked. "I've always been unhappy at work; I've always felt miserable and overwhelmed. I can't see myself as happy there." It was as if Lily had typecast herself into the role of depressed employee and felt doomed to play this role forever.

Lily, like others, confuses herself with her script. We've become attached to our scripts, and they have become integrated into our way of life and our way of looking at things. We think we are our scripts, so if we edit out part of our script, we think we are editing out a part of ourselves. This is a very frightening thought.

We *do* lose something when we let go of our old scripts. We lose an image of ourselves, as Lily felt, or we lose a hidden payoff. Ultimately, we lose some illusions. They are illusions because all the fears about hurting our parents or losing their approval are fantasies. They don't exist for real; they are movies of the mind. They are fantasies about what we imagine our parents might say or do in response to us.

It is important to remember that our fantasies are not really about our flesh-and-blood parents. Instead, our fantasies are about the parents we create and carry around inside our minds. Our internal, critical parents are usually far more powerful, and far more critical of us, than any real parent.

But illusions are powerful, and they provide comfort to us. To let go of them is to lose something; yet, you must let go to change. It is the only way you can move on. The old must make way for the new. This is the natural process of change. As Anatole France observed, "All changes, even the most longed for, have their melancholy, for what we leave behind us is a part of ourselves; we must die to one life before we can enter into another."

To let go, you first need to honor how the old scripts served you, then let them drop to the cutting room floor.

Honoring the Purpose of Your Scripts

It can be painful to recognize the purpose underlying our scripts, but don't think of yourself as wrong or stupid for how you were. Instead, honor your scripts and the role you played in writing your scripts. Honor that your child's mind was able to figure out a way to get what you needed. Recognize what a bright, resourceful person you were that you found a way to get your needs met. Now, as an adult, you can look for better ways to do that; you can handle things differently, but do honor the ingenious child in you who figured out a way to bring you to this point.

Honor your feelings. You don't have to act on them, but you want to own them. Until you do this, you cannot transcend them or change them. Respect the part of you that is frightened or feels that making a change is a daunting prospect. This frightened part is often the child inside you. Recognize and honor the resourceful child who coped, accommodated, adjusted, and survived.

Honor that your parents did their best for you, and that they could do no better than what they were taught or prepared to do. As adults, many of us continue to engage in struggles with our parents. Sometimes these struggles take place with them directly; often they take place in our minds. When you can acknowledge and honor your parents' good intentions, you can begin to let go of the struggle and the old scripts.

Letting Go of Old Scripts

Gabriella, who hesitated to be successful for fear of hurting her sister, needed to come to grips with her mother, Clara, and Clara's part in creating Gabriella's scripts. I helped her look at her past through the objective eye of the movie director. Gabriella saw that although her mother ran the family by guilt, she truly cared about her children. Facing limited financial resources after Gabriella's father died, Clara raised two small children alone. To Clara, her children's well-being was the most important goal in her life, even if her ways of expressing it were convoluted.

Gabriella came to understand that when her mother told her not to brag about her achievements, her intention was not to diminish Gabriella, but to protect her younger, less talented daughter from feeling inferior. Once Gabriella honored her mother's efforts and the strength it took to raise a family under difficult circumstances, she could change her script and her behavior. She could begin to act in her own best interests and work toward realizing her own goals and objectives. She couldn't do that when she was still reacting to her mother through her old scripts

Andy, the manager in a research firm, has difficulty in making decisions. He has come to realize that this stems from his belief that he must be perfect. He understands that he developed this belief in response to his highly critical parents who would never accept less than his best effort—and often wouldn't accept that. Like Gabriella, Andy realizes that his parents truly wanted the best for him. They believed they were motivating and helping him achieve his potential by pushing him to do better and not settling for second place.

To let go of his old script, with its irrational belief of perfection, Andy must separate himself from his parents and say goodbye to their influence. At the same time, he wants to acknowledge that they loved him and did their best to help him develop. He decided to write a letter to them. It was not a letter he planned to send; instead, it was a way for him to honor his parents, their scripts, and their best intentions formally, and to recognize the positive things they had done for him.

Russell, the doctor who wanted to be a musician, and Adele, who resisted her parent's pushing her to go to college, also needed to honor their parents. They needed to recognize that their parents only wanted what was best for them. They need to honor the loyal child inside them, a child who loves his or her family so much that he or she feels deep pain when not living in accordance with parental wishes.

For some, the hardest thing to give up is a cherished childhood fantasy that someone will come along to make everything better, or rescue them from difficult spots, just as their parents did, or as they wished their parents had done. This is frequently played out in the workplace when people rely on their unions, or on the human resources department, to be protective and intervene, sometimes for unreasonable causes.

Some people rescue themselves from difficult situations by getting sick. I'm not talking about catching the flu that is going around or the occasional illness. Instead, I mean responding to stressful work situations through habitual illness. Letting go of this response means recognizing and understanding the purpose of the script that calls for you to get sick in the face of stress. Being sick serves a purpose: it may temporarily relieve the pressure, buy some time, reduce expectations, or elicit sympathy from others. Once you recognize the purpose, it is time to look for different ways to handle stress, and find other ways to get the caring attention you crave. Being sick may have worked in your script as a child, when you felt powerless. Now, as an adult, you have more strength; you can handle conflicts in more empowered ways. You can tell yourself, "I can accept my need to get sick because I'm ready to examine what this coping mechanism is all about."

Loss and Your New Script

Scenarios for Success
Action
Exercise # 7-B

Sometimes it is difficult to put new scripts in place because you haven't acknowledged and mourned your losses.

- What do you think you will lose if you change your script?
- How will you deal with your loss?
- What do you think others will lose if you change your script?
- How will you help others deal with their loss?

You must be honest and acknowledge where you came from, what you have felt in the past, and what you are going through in the present as you recognize, acknowledge, and begin to change your scripts. Your scripts and the roles you have played have been an important part of your life. They have kept you safe and secure, connected you to your family, helped you win your parents' approval, and helped you find your place in the world.

Grieving

Change involves letting go of old ways, and it is appropriate to grieve for the loss of your old scripts or old illusions. Until you acknowledge what your losses are and mourn them, you may find it difficult to move forward.

When Reba came to see me, she had worked up her courage to leave a job where she felt stifled and unappreciated. Yet for several months after she had changed jobs, she found herself regretting her decision. Every time she heard about her former co-workers meeting for a group lunch or celebrating someone's birthday, she regretted leaving. It reminded her that she was no longer part of this work group, which triggered feelings of loss and sadness. She felt rejected because she wasn't invited to these get-togethers anymore. The feelings continued to gnaw at her, making it difficult for her to feel fully committed to her new job.

When Reba finally looked at her pain, she recognized she missed the warm camaraderie. Yet when she was honest, she also realized that as wonderful as those relationships had been, they were not enough to sustain her when she felt stuck in her old job. Her choice to move on had been a good one. Now she had to recognize what she had lost when she made the move. She could continue to feel rejected, or she could do something about it. She realized she could invite her former co-workers to join her for a drink after work. Once she did this, her regrets about her job change went away. She also found she could begin making connections with her new co-workers and form new relationships. Reba had to recognize and mourn the loss of all the wonderful years she had spent with this group of people before she could move on to fully accept her new life.

Sometimes people play the *if only* game with themselves. This is another movie we run in our minds, imagining how our lives would be different today *if only* we had done something differently or known something that we know now. Replaying the past is useful only if it helps you learn how to help yourself in the future. Replay the movie of the event, extract the lesson and wisdom from it, and then release it. It isn't real anymore. To make the changes in your scripts and to play the adult role in your life movie, you must learn from the past, plan for the future, but live in the present.

To continue to regret a past decision or a past action traps you in the role of *poor me,* the failure. The director in you has to say, "Cut! What's the lesson here? Learn the lesson and give me wisdom on the next take."

When you try to make a change for yourself, mourning what you lose is critical in order for you to enact the change and make it permanent. Often when you resist change in the workplace, you are doing so because you haven't mourned your losses.

Life is full of changes: starting school, leaving for college, starting a new job, getting married, having children, finding another job. Every change, even a change that you instigate, involves loss. You let go of something old to make room for something new. You let go of being a high school student to enter college. You let go of being a student when you started your first full-time job. You let go of the image of yourself as a single person when you enter into an exclusive romantic relationship or marriage. In making the changes I have been describing in this book, you must often let go of a cherished dream in your old scripts of how life ought to be. You have to lose something outdated to modernize your life.

Changes bring gains as well as losses, but sometimes you can't see your gains because you are focused only on your losses. Reynaldo is a union leader in a large medical center. A few years ago the hospital merged with another medical center, and duplicate functions were eliminated. Several of his co-workers lost their jobs. He was upset and felt powerless to do anything to save their jobs. He is still angry that they were laid off, and he feels guilty for having survived the cutbacks.

After the cutbacks, his job changed. He was given more responsibility, which he enjoys, but he is unwilling to acknowledge the gains he has made since the merger. He would be more successful if he let go of the anger and guilt he feels. Feeling powerless, he chooses instead to complain about the changes and grumble that the union is at the mercy of hospital management.

Reynaldo believes that if he acknowledges how he has benefited from the change, he will be abandoning the memory of his co-workers who lost their jobs. He holds tight to those memories, afraid to let go. Reynaldo needs to let go of the emotional grip the memories have on him, not the memories themselves. He is stuck in the past and ignoring the present, where he really needs to be.

Scenarios for Success

Action

Exercise # | 7 - C

Letting Go of the Past

Sometimes when you are unable to let go of your outdated scripts, it is because you are still holding onto old resentments, hurts, or unfulfilled dreams from the past. When they are painful, you may have buried them deep in your mind, and you may not be aware you are still harboring them. Yet they still paralyze you and impede your progress. Use the following exercise to identify old resentments, hurts, and lost dreams. Think back into your childhood history as far as you can.

• I never forgave _____ for _____.

• I have not recovered from _____. When that happened, I lost _____.

• If only I hadn't _____. I lost _____.

• If only he or she hadn't _____. When they did that, I lost _____.

• My mother never _____.

• My father never _____.

• My sister never _____.

• My brother never _____.

• Other significant people (identify who) never _____.

• I regret that I've never fulfilled my dream (or expectation) of

_____.

Once you have acknowledged these things, the grieving can start. You then can let go and move forward.

To move on, Reynaldo must acknowledge his losses, recognize why they were important to him, then let go of them emotionally. This is the mourning process. Mourning also involves accepting that things will never be the same as they were. Too many people dwell in the past, struggling with their losses without mourning. Refusing to mourn keeps the past alive. By mourning, you take a giant step toward managing the anxiety that accompanies change, and you rejoin the present.

Staying Focused on Change

Any change involves a tradeoff. You let go of one thing, and something new replaces it. To grab onto something new, you need to let go of something old. In between the passing off, though, there is a transitional period, that awkward time when you become aware that the familiar old script doesn't work anymore, but the new script isn't comfortable for you yet.

We sometimes need to buoy ourselves up to remember why we wanted to change in the first place. During transitions, people often focus on what they are losing. Optimism serves you well during times of change, and focusing on what you will gain in a positive way keeps you motivated. A huge gain is that you will feel empowered rather than victimized, energetic and upbeat rather than drained and stuck, satisfied rather than frustrated, positive about yourself and about life rather than gloomy and full of self-loathing.

Good questions to ask yourself at this point are: "Why do I want to change this behavior?" and "What will be the benefits or payoffs?" Focusing on the positive benefits of the change and on what you will gain will help keep you motivated to continue to use the new scripts.

It can also help to have the support of successful people you trust as you change your scripts and implement new behaviors. Some people enlist the aid of a spouse, co-worker or close friend they trust to act as a coach to help them as they make changes in their scripts. You can say to this person, "Remind me how miserable I've been and why I said I wanted to change." One woman who was trying to break her pattern of playing the victim asked a co-worker she trusted to remind her when she started whining.

One word of advice here, however: choose people who support your changes rather than those who might want you to stay as you are. It is best to select a mentor figure, someone who already exemplifies the person you want to be like.

Replacements

You can write a new script of how you want to be, but you can't act it with conviction until you have replaced what you are giving up with something else. Changing your scripts does not mean you have to lose the connection you have to your parents. Instead, it means finding a way to maintain the connection that does not force you to limit your ability to succeed.

Vivien's manager told her she was being considered for a promotion she had been working to get, but she had undermined her chances for success in the past, and she feared she would do it again. The closer she got to achieving her goals, the more she would drink. One cocktail before dinner became two or three. In two previous jobs, her drinking had affected her ability to get up and get to work on time with a clear head. She began to fear she was about to slip down this same path again.

Through coaching, Vivien took a hard, objective look at what drinking represented to her. When she thought about having a drink after work, she thought about her parents. Her earliest memory of alcohol was watching her father fix a martini when she was five. Pondering the memory, she recalled that her parents always had a cocktail after work. Her father mixed the drinks in the kitchen and carried them out to the living room where her mother was stretched out luxuriously on the sofa, her stockinged feet resting on the sofa arm. Vivien recalled how she sat with them as they relaxed and joked, and they seemed warm and loving to her. The times she felt most safe and secure as a child were when she sat laughing with them as they drank their cocktails and she nibbled the olives her mother plucked from her drinks.

The idea of starting a new job excited Vivien, but it scared her as well. To ease her anxieties and feel comforted, Vivien enacted what her parents had modeled for her. She had a cocktail to start the evening to feel relaxed and mellow. Sipping her drink evoked the unconscious memories of feeling glamorous, safe, and secure. In her scripts, written during childhood, drinking created a feeling that *the world is a wonderful place and I'm just fine.*

Giving up evening cocktails felt to Vivien like giving up her parents. Drinking was her connection to them, yet it was a connection that had a negative impact in her life today. She needed to connect with them emotionally, rather than through her drinking behavior. She decided to create a scrapbook of her memories of her parents. She gathered photographs of them and other souvenirs from childhood. Creating the scrapbook helped her feel connected with her parents and reminded her that she had options other than drinking when she felt anxious. She could recall the warm relaxed feelings by looking though her scrapbook.

Marcus also needed to replace his family connection. He had left his family and home town when he won a college scholarship. Despite his parents' wishes for him to return after completing graduate school, Marcus chose to move across the country to pursue career opportunities. While building a successful career, he was haunted by feelings of having lost a connection with his family, his community, and his heritage.

When Marcus read about a literacy program seeking volunteers at his local library, he called immediately and signed up. Sharing his time teaching children and adults to read in a community similar to his home town became his way both to contribute to his community and to honor his heritage. Perhaps you, like Marcus, can find an activity that helps you connect with your losses so that you can move on.

Change isn't always easy, and letting go of well-practiced and familiar scripts affects us at a very deep, emotional level. Yet once you figure out why you are stuck, it is easier to move on and bring to life your new scripts for success.

Change is also a non-stop process. You are always cutting and revising your script. When you are in pain, you will most likely change your script as a healing measure, but as you become adept at the process, you may make changes to give extra power to *My Successful Career*.

Chapter 8

Actor's Workshop
Acting Your Successful New Role

The best actors in show business truly relish the opportunity to take on a challenging script. They like being able to jump into a character's shoes and explore that person from the inside out. To give a convincing performance, they have to be able to see life from their character's point of view. They have to understand how that person thinks and feels. They have to know why that character behaves as he or she does. Learning about the intricacies of a character is the hard part. Once they have the character firmly implanted in their mind, they can become that character and deliver a convincing performance.

For your starring role in *My Successful Career*, you've been taking a director's viewpoint and looking at your life through new eyes. We have worked on understanding the scripts you wrote during childhood, and we have re-written those scripts. We have dealt with letting go of old beliefs, which can be a difficult and time-consuming process. Beliefs are so firmly embedded and are such a deep part of you that changing them requires a very concerted effort with lots of rehearsing.

We talked previously about how, when you change a belief, your thoughts, feelings, and behavior change to align with that new belief. Ultimately, your behavior is what other people judge and respond to. Your beliefs, thoughts, and feelings are internal factors, while your behavior is external. Often you can keep your thoughts and feelings secret, but your behavior is visible to the world. Sometimes you need to make immediate changes in your behavior to make the biggest impact at work.

In comparison to changing your beliefs, changing your behavior is relatively easy. It's said that, with intention and practice, you can change a habit in three weeks. Behaviors are habits, so you should be able to change them in a short time. Once you are focused clearly on your intention, practice merging those behaviors into your new script. If you were an actor in a real movie, you would soon be thinking, feeling, and acting that new script. In *My Successful Career*, the life you are acting out is the best one you can give yourself.

Your Behavior Can Sabotage You

We have seen how we sabotage ourselves with unproductive thinking and feelings. We can also behave in ways that sabotage our best intentions. Nora, the information security consultant, has the best interests of her clients at heart; yet her behavior—yelling at people, accusing them of incompetence, interrupting them as they speak, and refusing to listen to their explanations—serves neither the client's interests nor her own. She has developed a reputation for being unprofessional, difficult, and a "drama queen." She has just been put on formal warning for being verbally abusive to one of her clients. While Nora works on changing her pessimistic outlook and her belief that she is unworthy, she needs to change her behavior immediately to avoid further disciplinary action.

Making such behavioral changes requires calling upon the director's advice and insights. A director would look at Nora's situation and ask, "What does Nora have to do to get what she wants?"

To make changes in your behavior, you again need to pull back from your situation as you did in changing your thoughts and feelings. Look at it through the objective lens of the camera. This diverts your attention from your feelings and directs it to your behavior. You want your focus solely on your behavior; if you focus on your feelings, you may feel scared and start to think of how hard it is to change. The wheels of negativity keep spinning. You begin thinking of all the things you're not good at and overwhelm yourself with feelings of hopelessness. Meanwhile, you stay stuck. The solution is to yell, "Cut!" Stop the distressing thoughts and feelings and get into action. Your actions—your behaviors—are what you want to change right now.

People I coach often continue repeating the same unsuccessful behaviors even though those behaviors have never produced the results they want. "So, let's see," I said to a client, "Every week for the past several months you've been asking your boss, 'When are you going to give me a new assignment?'

She's always told you to be patient. Now your requests irritate her more. Do you really think if you ask her again in the same way that you've been asking her for months that she'll react in a different way?"

If what you do doesn't work the way you want, don't persist in doing it exactly the same way over and over. I coach my clients to try something different. Challenge the behaviors that aren't working for you. Like our beliefs, our behaviors become embedded. But if they aren't getting the results you want, look for alternative behaviors.

Change Your Behavior

You can use the Director's Challenge described in chapter five to examine your behavior in situations in which what you do or say prevents you from getting the results you want.

When you are in situations that you feel you have not handled well or that have not turned out the way you would like, play the part of the director. Look at what you have been doing and ask yourself these questions:

- Has my behavior achieved my intended results?
- Is my behavior appropriate for a mature, successful professional?
- If I continue this behavior, will it get me the results I want?
- What actions can I take that are appropriate for a successful professional and will give me the results I want?

Generate as many potential alternatives as possible on different ways you could handle the situation. Be creative here and get past familiar responses and your traditional ways of thinking. You have to look beyond your old scripts.

You might find it helpful to talk to a colleague or friend whom you trust. They can help you look at the situation and point out what behaviors don't work for you. They can also suggest options for alternative behaviors.

Andy is the research firm manager who delayed making decisions for fear that he would be seen as an imperfect manager. He knew he had to change his belief that he was not okay unless he was perfect. Meanwhile, when he put on his director's cap and scrutinized his behavior, he saw that his reluctance to make quick decisions prompted both senior management and his staff to see him as a poor manager.

When I challenged him to find ways to make decisions more quickly, he decided he could set a decision-making deadline and commit to it whether or not he thought he had all the information that might exist. He also could create a simple decision table and jot down all possible options; in this way he could write pro and con factors for each option to help him decide what to do.

Andy realized the most difficult decisions were those in which there were no clear-cut answers, even when he used a decision table. He asked Raj, a colleague he admired and trusted, how he made decisions. Raj said he used a 60–40 rule on close decisions. "In these cases, it's impossible to be 100 percent sure that something is the right decision," Raj told him. "If I'm at least 60 percent sure of one course of action, I go with that. And I tell myself it's the best decision based on what I know today. I'm willing to take the risk and to deal with the consequences."

"What if you get information later that shows another option would have been better?"

"Then you deal with it," Raj said. "It's like referees in a ball game. They don't have time to weigh the pros and cons of every decision. They have to make their best call so the game can continue. You have to do the same. Make your best call, based on what you know today, then move on. If you find out later something else would have been better, you learn from it and see how it affects future decisions. That's what being a manager is all about: taking intelligent risks and sometimes making mistakes. Just remember that they don't pay you to be perfect; they pay you to be productive."

The next morning, when Andy was faced with an issue, he gave himself until 5 P.M. to make a decision. He found that using the decision table helped rescue him from the emotional sea and turned decision-making into a logical, analytical process. The hardest part was controlling his anxiety about making bad decisions. When it welled up, he thought of Raj's analogy of a referee. The referee image helped Andy let go of the urge to be perfect.

Andy continued to apply his new decision-making behaviors. He still felt anxious each time, but he soon saw the positive results of his new behavior. One of his employees, Anita, told him, "You surprised me the other day! I asked you where we stood on the Miller project, and I expected you to waffle, but you told me exactly what you had decided. That was great. We're really moving forward on that project now." Andy realized how his indecisiveness in the past had delayed his staff and had impaired productivity and eroded morale.

Use a Role Model

Observing how people you know and admire handle situations can give you ideas for alternate ways to respond and behave. Just as young actors learn tips and techniques from experienced actors, you can learn from others how to be successful in dealing with situations in the workplace.

Tanya sometimes found herself overwhelmed in handling her new responsibilities as a benefits coordinator for an insurance company. She found it helpful to use her boss, Elena, as a role model. Tanya said, "When I face tough situations and start to feel scared, I say to myself, 'Now, what would Elena do?' Then I do whatever I think she would do. Imagining how she would do it takes my focus off my negative thoughts and puts it on solving the problem."

Tanya's technique is effective because it immediately takes her out of the irrational, scared-child mode of thinking and pops her into a rational, logical adult frame of mind. It gives her the distance she needs to examine the situation and come up with a new, productive response. Tanya may think she is simply imitating her boss's response. In fact, she is drawing upon her own adult resources to handle the situation appropriately and effectively.

You may look at how others handle similar situations and think, "Oh, well, it's easy for them. They don't have to deal with the problems I have." True, they don't have *exactly* the same problems you have, but that doesn't mean they aren't coping with other difficulties. What objective evidence do you have that it's easy for them?

Some years ago, when I worked as an employee assistance counselor for a large company, I counseled two women who were colleagues in the audit department. Neither knew that that the other was seeing me. Zoe was a successful auditor plagued with personal and family problems. Her alcoholic husband, who was in denial, needed treatment for his problem or he would lose his job. Her teenage son was failing most of his classes in school; her mother, who had been battling cancer for two years, had taken a turn for the worse. Zoe sought help on how to handle these issues; she didn't want them to interfere with her work responsibilities.

Her colleague, Mary Ann, came to me for coaching on how to correct her inappropriate behaviors at work that affected her job performance. Her manager had complained she made too many personal calls at work, was frequently absent, and was having problems focusing on her assignments. She was letting her personal life intrude into her job.

In one of our meetings, I asked Mary Ann to choose a successful role model she could emulate to inspire her when she struggled. She chose Zoe, whom she felt represented a successful corporate woman. Mary Ann thought that it was easy for Zoe to give her all to her job. When I asked her to explain, She said, "Zoe earns a great salary, so she can hire people to help her around the house and take care of her kids. She has a wonderful, supportive husband. It's easy for her because she doesn't have my obstacles." I thought, "If Mary Ann only knew!"

Unless you have hard evidence to the contrary, it is not accurate to assume that people who are successful and happy in their jobs have no problems of their own. Successful people often struggle with problems, but they have found ways to overcome their problems so that they can be successful. As we saw with optimists, most successful people compartmentalize problems; they don't let problems interfere with every aspect of their jobs. Excusing yourself by saying others don't have to face the obstacles you do simply keeps you stuck in the same place.

When You Need to Change Immediately

What happens in situations where you need to change your behavior immediately? For example, suppose you and your manager are discussing a presentation you gave the day before. Your manager begins to criticize the way you handled questions from the audience. You feel your jaw clenching and your chest tightening. Usually you respond to criticism by becoming defensive and sullen, yet you know that it would be better—and certainly more professional—to open yourself to hearing your manager's comments. You don't have the luxury to take a break and do exercises from this book; you need to perform a new role on the spot.

We have talked previously about how you can say "Cut!" at any moment to stop your negative thoughts and feelings. You also can say "Cut!" at any moment to stop your behavior and change it instantaneously.

As you have done during other changes, call on your inner director to help you detach and look at the scene differently. Imagine you are looking at the scene through the camera lens. Sometimes it helps in examining scenes such as this to sit in the director's chair. By this, I mean shift your position. Get up and sit in a different place. Stand and walk around. Change your position in your chair. Shifting your body can give you a new view of the situation and remove you from a body posture—such as slouching or hunching your shoulders—that reinforces your old scripts.

As you examine the scene, stay in the present tense. Don't slide into past history or project into the future. Separate *then* from *now*. When the old scripts and the old reels start running, say "Cut!" Keep yourself focused on what you need to do here and now. A good question to keep asking yourself is, "What do I need to do right now to get the results I want?"

You may wonder how you can possibly think like a director during a rapidly unfolding situation when your emotions are gushing like a broken water main. It may sound complex to you, but slipping into the director role can happen quickly and easily once you have practiced it. It becomes familiar, almost automatic, just like any other habit. Learn how to put your director on call.

Remember Tanya, the insurance benefits coordinator, who thinks of her boss Elena to help her deal with a difficult situation? She asks herself, "Now, what would Elena do?" This valuable technique helps her detach and put the new behaviors quickly in place. If you have a role model, think of what that person would do, then do it.

The Impact of Behavior Changes

I tell my clients, "If your behavior isn't getting you the results you want, then change your behavior. New behavior brings new results." Do something different—something positive—even if at first you don't fully believe it will work. Try something different just to see if you will get a different result. If the new behavior yields the results you want, a wonderful thing starts to happen: the change in your behavior changes your feelings, and when your feelings change, your beliefs also eventually change to be in alignment with the feelings.

Simone discovered the power of making just one small change. She consistently prefaced her suggestions and ideas by saying, "This is probably a stupid idea, but . . . " If her idea was well received, Simone would laugh and say, "Oh, it's nothing. You could have thought of it." Her behavior resulted from pessimistic thinking, from her belief that she wasn't as smart as her co-workers. Unfortunately, her behavior made it easy for others to grab her ideas and run with them without acknowledging Simone's creative contributions.

Once she caught on, Simone became angry that she didn't get credit for her ideas. Her colleague, Annie, pointed out to Simone that her self-deprecating comments diminished the value of her contributions and undercut her power. Annie suggested that Simone introduce her ideas by saying, "Here's my idea," instead of making a value judgment about it. Though doubtful,

Simone agreed to give it a try. She discovered that by following Annie's advice she felt more confident about her idea and could acknowledge her creativity for herself. She continued doing it, and she noticed changes in how she felt about herself. She found she could accept compliments more graciously by saying "Thank you," instead of "It was nothing."

You have probably had an experience like this yourself. Think about a time when you didn't know how to do something and weren't sure you would ever be able to do it competently. Perhaps the first time you started using a computer you thought, "This looks scary and hard. I don't think I can do it." You took a computer class, perhaps reluctantly, and you went through the motions the instructor described. By the end of the class, you were using the computer and found out it wasn't so difficult after all. Your feelings about using a computer changed for the better. Through your actions, your thoughts and feelings changed. Your successful actions become evidence to support new thoughts and new feelings.

We have seen that when you change your beliefs, everything else that follows—your thoughts, feelings, and behaviors—will change. The reverse is also true: if you change your behavior, your feelings, your thoughts and, eventually, your beliefs will change as well.

Do It Even if You Don't Feel Like It

We make excuses for not changing our behavior. We say, "I'll do it differently next time . . . when I am less stressed . . . when things are going better . . . when I feel better about myself." Many of us make the mistake of thinking that we have to feel a certain way before we can act a certain way. For example, you might think, "I have to feel calm and confident before I can go up to a stranger and introduce myself at a business function. I have to feel completely confident that I have all the facts available before I can make a decision. I have to feel like creating the spreadsheet before I can start to work on it. I have to feel like I really know what I'm doing before I can attempt anything."

This kind of thinking is irrational and holds you back from doing things. It's possible to do things without feeling like you are ready to do them. Think about the times you don't feel like doing something, but you do it anyway. If we never did anything unless we felt like doing it, many chores would never get done. You do these things even if you don't feel like doing them because you know the consequences you will suffer if you don't do them.

Focus on the Goal

What helps a marathon runner get through the last grueling miles when her feet feel like lead, her legs wobble like rubber, and each breath is a strain? When she feels she can't run another step, why does she push on? The marathon runner focuses on the goal: she sees herself running across the finish line and imagines the triumphant feeling she will enjoy. How does someone who works a stressful, full-time job leave the office fatigued at day's end and still find the energy to go to class at night? He, too, focuses on his goal: a better paying job and the great feeling of having earned his MBA.

People like these keep their eyes riveted on their goals. This is what helps them get through the rough spots when they don't feel like continuing. This same technique can work for you. What are your goals? What will be the payoffs for your new behavior? Focus on the feelings of success and accomplishment that you will enjoy when you are acting in a way that produces success.

Acting "As If"

It can be scary to do things differently before your feelings and beliefs are aligned. It takes a leap of faith that acting differently will produce the results you want. During this time, you need to act *as if*. Act *as if* you are already patient, *as if* you are already unafraid, *as if* you can make decisions easily.

Sometimes, when directing people in a film, the director says, "Even if you don't feel the emotion, I want you to act as if you do." Going through the motions, like a rehearsal, helps you develop the confidence you need to make the new behaviors an established part of your repertoire.

Charlotte always dreaded going to trade shows where her company displayed its latest products. She felt uncomfortable around people she didn't know. "I'm so shy around strangers," she said to her colleague, June. "I don't know how to talk to people. I'm afraid they'll think I'm an idiot."

June suggested Charlotte make a game of talking to people at the show. "Don't think about being shy," she told Charlotte. "Instead, imagine you're a famous anthropologist. Your job is to interview seven people to find out who they are."

It didn't sound very exciting to Charlotte, but she was willing to give it a try. Pretending to be a famous anthropologist took her focus off her feelings and transferred it to her behavior. She thought about the questions an anthropologist would ask to learn about the people she met. Taking a deep breath, she stepped deeper into the role and walked up to the first person she saw who looked friendly. To her delight, he was pleasant, and Charlotte found it easy to ask her marketing-related questions. The second person was even easier to talk to, and by the end of the day, Charlotte had chatted with dozens of people. Success spun off of success, in part because of the role she had acted.

Charlotte actually used a method that actors use. By performing the actions that a character would perform, the actor appears believable as the character. As Charlotte discovered, acting as if she were comfortable striking up conversations with others inspired those people to respond to her as if she really were a poised and capable conversationalist. By using this method, she created her own self-fulfilling prophecy.

Charlotte's success at the trade show helped her create a new script for herself. Previously, she had acquired plenty of evidence that she couldn't talk to strangers. She could draw upon years of negative experiences; she could recall trade shows, company parties, and conferences where she was in a room full of strangers and was afraid to talk to anyone. To change her script, she needed evidence to challenge and dispute this notion. Her success at meeting and talking to people at the latest trade show helped her compile positive evidence to show she was successful at speaking to strangers. "I guess I really can't say I'm shy if I can talk to strangers," she beamed. Actual successes finally changed her belief and, ultimately, her script.

Even with her new script, Charlotte still felt anxious about introducing herself to strangers. Whenever that happened, she focused on her feelings of success from the trade show and found she could dispel the anxiety. She continued to practice what she came to call the "anthropologist technique" to build a new string of successes, each one reinforcing her new script. When she chose to act as if she were comfortable talking to strangers, she found she could talk to anyone.

Focus on the Good Feelings

Charlotte inadvertently discovered a technique that helps many people be successful. By choosing to focus on the good feelings of being a success rather than the negative feelings of failing, she could be successful.

Another technique is to use your success in one endeavor to help you be successful in other endeavors. When you carry over the positive feelings of success from one area into another area, you keep your focus on being successful, and you quiet the nagging voice of the internal critic that unconsciously holds you back. Charlotte, for example, was very good at analyzing proposals from vendors, and her manager often complimented her on her analytical skills. She could choose to focus on her feelings of success when she analyzed proposals, and maintain that positive feeling when she walked into a room full of strangers.

Practice and Rehearse Your New Scripts

As with any new skill, new behaviors take practice. It usually feels awkward to act in unfamiliar ways. "It doesn't feel right—it doesn't feel like me," you may complain. Of course it doesn't—it's not you yet! You're still writing your new script and auditioning parts of it. Until it is more familiar, it will feel strange. In some situations, you can create an opportunity to rehearse new behaviors before you debut them. Plan for some temporary discomfort while you learn the new role. If you feel like giving up, recall how much misery your old ways caused you, then consider how much better off you will be with success. The eventual outcome of pushing your way through the temporary discomfort is success and a positive self-image.

Distressed about being put on warning for screaming at a client, Nora knew she had to change. She knew her beliefs did not serve her, and she had to revise them, but in the meantime, she needed to alter her behavior right away or risk further disciplinary action.

She assumed the role of the director to determine what she needed to do, and she made a list of specific actions she could take. She knew that she often wallowed in self-pity when she felt the world was against her. She resolved to say, "Cut! Self-pity stinks!" to herself whenever she started feeling neglected, rejected, angry, or hurt. This phrase blasted her out of her emotional turmoil and into her intellect. Then she could objectively determine the best steps to take.

To keep herself focused, present, and objective, she resolved to take a deep breath and imagine herself backing away from the situation and standing behind a camera to view it. I suggested she imagine spraying herself with a coat of Teflon before meeting with her clients so that other people's opinions, attitudes, and judgments would slide off her. Finally, she resolved to listen to others without speaking and to count to five before she spoke in response. Nora wrote down these ideas for changing her behaviors. Her list became a reminder of her resolutions she could review before meeting with clients.

To help implement the new behaviors, Nora used a visualization technique many championship athletes use to prepare before a competition. They play a mental movie in which they see themselves performing perfectly. They imagine themselves racing down the ski slope and leaning into the curve around each gate, or they see themselves skating flawlessly, hitting each jump and landing surely on foot, or swinging a baseball bat smoothly and smacking the ball into the upper deck. This visualization serves as a practice or a rehearsal. Nora played her mental movie, and she saw herself going through the steps—saying "self-pity stinks," breathing, detaching, spraying herself with imaginary Teflon, and remaining quiet for several seconds before speaking.

While these actions helped Nora, the new behaviors weren't easy for her at first. They took deliberate effort, planning, and persistence. When her manager questioned one of her reports, she immediately thought, "He hates me and wants to fire me!" Then she countered that negative thought and said to herself, "Cut! That's not a helpful thought. I have no evidence he is thinking that."

The first few times she met with clients to discuss security controls, she had to bite her lip to keep from interrupting and yelling when they offered what she considered were lame excuses for not implementing the controls she had recommended. Yet each meeting became easier as she continued to practice her new behaviors, and the practice made the actions more comfortable and more familiar.

Nora also began keeping a journal, in which she wrote down all the times she had used one of the new behaviors each day. Reviewing the journal helped her see how she was progressing in changing her behavior. This positive reinforcement boosted her self-esteem.

As Nora continued to use the new behaviors, she became less defensive, less reactive, and a better listener. Her co-workers changed, too. They responded more favorably to her. They began to ask her for advice and to see her as a valuable resource. Nora thrived on the acceptance and positive feedback. Other people's positive responses to her became the evidence she needed to convince herself that she was a worthy person and that people liked her. Her beliefs and feelings shifted to be in alignment with her changed behavior. She had passed through a period of discomfort to put her new behaviors in place, but eventually, through practice and persistence, they became her familiar routine.

Changing a Specific Behavior

To change a specific behavior, you first identify what you want to change. Then you brainstorm on the specific steps you will take to put the new behavior in place. For example, here are common behaviors my clients wanted to change and some of the strategies they developed for changing them:

Behavior to change: Being resentful.
Desired behavior: Cooperate with my team members.
Specific steps to implement new behavior:
    I will go beyond the scope of my job.
    I will refer people to someone else if I can't help them.
    I will exhibit a positive can-do attitude.
    I will over-deliver.
    I will pitch in on tasks and do whatever it takes to get the job done.
Positive rewards:
    My manager will be pleased that I'm turning my performance around.
    I will get positive feedback from co-workers.
    My co-workers will be more cooperative.
    If I want to apply for another position in the company, I will get a good recommendation.
    I may get a better performance review.

Behavior to change: Being tardy.
Desired behavior: Arrive at least fifteen minutes early for work every day this month.
Specific steps to implement new behavior:
    I will prepare my clothes for the next day before I go to bed.
    I will put my keys by the front door.
    I will prepare my children's lunches the night before.
    I will leave by 7:30 to catch the 7:45 bus.
Positive rewards:
    I will feel calm and ready to start the day instead of feeling frazzled.
    I will have plenty of time to arrange my assignments for the day.
    I will be on time for early-morning meetings.
    My manager will stop nagging me and looking at her watch when I arrive.
    My manager won't put me on warning for being late.

Behavior to change: Bringing my bad moods in to work.

Desired behavior: Have a positive, upbeat attitude at work.

Specific steps to implement new behavior:

> I will focus on optimism and remember that good things happen often.
>
> I will renew my commitment to care about what happens at work.
>
> I will be cordial to everyone I speak with.
>
> When I feel myself slipping, I will take a deep breath, count to ten and visualize pleasant memories.
>
> I will smile when I answer the phone.

Positive rewards:

> My co-workers will talk to me more often.
>
> I will be appreciated and supported by others.
>
> I will be more confident and optimistic when I act *as if.*
>
> I will feel like a member of the team.
>
> I will be invited to lunches and after-work gatherings.

You can apply successful strategies such as these for any behavior you want to change.

Keep a Success Journal

Like Nora, you may also find it helpful to keep a journal of your progress in changing your behavior. Keeping a *success journal* can help you say on track, motivated, and in character as you work on changing your behavior. Think of this journal as both a response to the director's notes and as a progress report. In a notebook, write down everything you have done today that brings you closer to establishing the new behavior. Did you try something you have never tried before? Write that down in your journal. Did you try acting *as if*? Write that down, too. How did it feel to do that—was it comfortable, scary, thrilling, confusing? Write down the feelings you experienced. Also include your thoughts, ideas, and any insights into your scripts that occur to you.

Review your journal every evening. This review is like a meeting of the actor and the director to discuss the day's work. Give yourself credit for all the little steps you took during the day. Each step brings you that much closer to changing your habits or behavior. Note also how you feel about the changes you are making. Acknowledge and own all the feelings: discomfort, sadness, fear, worry, pride, self-satisfaction, or a sense of accomplishment. Acknowl-

Scenarios for Success

Action

Exercise # | 8-A

Change Your Workplace Behavior

Choose a behavior you want to change in the workplace and strategize on the steps you will take to change it. You may want to review the strategies described in the examples on the previous page. On a piece of paper, write down your answers to these questions.

- What is the behavior you want to change?
- How do you want to act?
- What are the specific steps you need to take to change this behavior?
- Who can you use as a role model for the behavior you want to have?
- What rewards will you enjoy when you change the behavior?

edging the negative feelings helps you get through them. Focusing on the positive feelings will help you increase them.

Ask For What You Want

If we don't ask for what we want, we probably won't get it. Susan Jeffers, author of *Feel the Fear and Do It Anyway*, says fear prevents us from making changes and going after what we really desire. We often fear asking for what we want because we fear we will be rejected; yet, again, if you act as if you are confident, you are more likely to get what you want.

You cannot expect other people to know what you need or want unless you tell them. Remember, they are starring in their own movies and are working from their own scripts; they aren't thinking about your movie, your scripts, and your needs. For example, Mishi frequently felt angry because her boss,

Paul, often stepped into her office with requests or tasks at 5:30 P.M. while she was preparing to leave to pick up her son. She knew her anger resulted from her feeling that Paul did not respect her schedule. At the same time, she realized she had never told him that such end-of-day requests created problems for her and that the requests and tasks could be handled easily the next morning. If she didn't set the limit, how could she expect anyone else to do so?

Mishi thought about how best to approach Paul to explain her situation and to come up with another way to handle his requests. She wrote down what she would say to him, and then she tried it out with a co-worker who knew Paul and could suggest how he might respond. The rehearsal helped Mishi put aside her anger so that she could work on stating the problem and providing a possible solution in clear, direct terms, free of accusations and defensiveness.

Mishi chose a quiet time to talk to Paul so that neither would be distracted by other problems. She spoke in a matter-of-fact manner. "Paul, there's something bothering me I would like to talk about. When I'm getting ready to leave for the day and you come into my office and you ask me to do something, it creates a problem for me. I understand that your request is important, and I want to help you. However, I need to leave on time so I can pick up my son. I would like to suggest we try something different: how about if I check in with you every day at five o'clock to see if there's anything you need me to do first thing in the morning. That way, I won't be distracted and worried about leaving on time, and you will know that you have my undivided attention."

Paul listened quietly as Mishi spoke and then said, "I had no idea I was creating a problem for you. I've come to your office at the end of the day because I know I can find you so I can talk to you." Mishi was surprised to hear Paul's perspective. It helped her realize that Paul had dozens of things on his mind and to expect him to tune in to her needs was unrealistic. Paul continued, "I like your idea. Let's start this afternoon."

What are the things that you want from others? What will you do to get those things? Can you ask for what you want from others in a direct, adult fashion instead of trying to get it through devious, childlike means?

Many of us want acknowledgement for our achievements. It is realistic to ask for it directly. Jayne worked for a boss, Daryl, who never praised his staff, but only told them what they had done wrong. She tried dropping hints. She tried embarrassing him by asking him in front of other employees, "When are we going to have our performance reviews so we can find out what we're doing right?" When this didn't work, Jayne realized she needed to ask Daryl directly for what she wanted.

One day, as they were talking about her work on a project, she said to him, "Daryl, you're very good at telling me what areas I need to improve in. However, I'd also like to hear from you what areas you think I do well in. It would be very motivating for me to know what you value in me." To her astonishment, Daryl proceeded to describe several areas in which he believed Jayne excelled, and he concluded by saying that he considered her one of his most valuable employees.

It never occurred to Daryl to give positive feedback to his employees because, according to his scripted beliefs, a manager's job is to point out what is wrong to help keep employees on track. He also felt that he would be perceived as being "soft" if he complimented his employees. Regardless of his script, Jayne had to find a way to get her needs met, and she discovered the best way was to ask directly for what she wanted.

What things do you want? Be truthful: do you want your boss to tell you that you are great? Do you want your co-workers to like you? Do you want to be invited to all the department lunches even if you don't attend all of them? Do you want to be asked for your opinion?

You have to own up to these needs and desires, and you have to look at where they come from. When you tell the truth about what you want, you suddenly realize that you are hearing the voice of your younger self. As we become adults, we learn to disown the part of ourselves that wants and needs things, particularly that part that wants attention. We learn to think that such desires are childish; we disown the part of ourselves that has these needs.

We may have adult bodies, but we still have feelings and needs from our childhood. We are being dishonest with ourselves if we deny this. In many cases, they really aren't childish needs—they are human needs. So make a list of your needs, and determine the best way to satisfy them.

The wise manager will recognize that most employees desire acknowledgment and will use compliments as powerful motivating tools. Not everyone is fortunate to work for such a manager, however. Rather than bemoaning that your boss never says positive things, you could be like Jayne and ask your manager for positive feedback. You could ask a co-worker whose opinion you trust and value to give you feedback, too.

You could also keep your own running list of your accomplishments. Instead of relying on others for feedback, you could refer to this list whenever you need a boost and a reminder of your successes. In fact, such a list could be useful in your performance review to remind your manager what you have accomplished during the review period.

You can change your behavior to get the results you want. When you see that your positive actions yield success, you see that you no longer have to cling to your old childhood scripts. You can get what you want, and feel better about your choices, by using adult behaviors that are appropriate for the twenty-first century workplace and for who you are today, the star of *My Successful Career.*

Chapter 9

A Work in Progress
Producing *My Successful Career*

Unlike movies you see at the theater, which are finished products, *My Successful Career* is a work in progress. Unlike a movie, which is frozen in time, your life continues. There's never a final version because you keep on living, growing, and changing.

Many people have the illusion that when we become adults, we are supposed to be finished products. Our major learning and growing is behind us, we think, and so are the struggles of childhood. I've had clients believe that when they finished therapy, they were supposed to be done with the problems they had been working on. They felt they would never again experience the distressing, negative feelings that brought them to therapy in the first place.

The truth is that you are never done. You never finish rewriting your scripts and refining your roles. Each day you can continue taking steps to change old scripts and break out of old habits that no longer serve you. Now you have the tools to deal with situations that cause you pain. You recognize the feelings that come up; you investigate to understand what has activated them. You rewrite your script to create the character you want to play and embody the feelings and behaviors you direct.

Continue to Refine and Revise

Continue refining your scripts. What script do you want to use for handling projects with tight deadlines? What script do you want to use for making decisions? What script do you want to use for dealing with being overlooked or ignored at work? After handling a tough situation with your new script, ask yourself, "Did I do it the way I wanted to? What might work better?" Call upon your director to help you determine where you can improve next time.

Nora, for example, now reviews each interaction she has with people to see how she handled herself. If it didn't go quite as smoothly as she would have liked, she puts on her director's hat and asks herself a series of questions: Did I remember to spray myself with Teflon? Could I have waited longer before speaking? Did I connect with the other person's concerns and not just focus on my own? Nora loves adding daily items to her success journal to celebrate all her progress.

It is a joy for me to run into clients I haven't seen in a year or two. I will ask them, "How is it going?" and with a grin, they will say, "Everything's just fine." They have forgotten what a beast of a problem they wrestled with in the past because their new scripts are working wonderfully for them now. They started with making a small change, and the success of that change encouraged them to keep making changes. Eventually, they had their new scripts in place. When we forget about those changes and take new habits for granted, we know we have integrated the new scripts into our lives.

Enhancing Quality

When you are comfortable with your new scripts, take the next step and look at how you can enhance the quality of your life even more. When I talk about quality, I mean having the kind of job and life that truly satisfies you.

Here are the questions to ask yourself as you look at how you can enhance the quality of your life:
- What is it you really want in a job?
- What is your personal vision? Think about the nature of the work you would like to do.
- What types of relationships would you like to have with your manager and co-workers?
- What kinds of rewards—both tangible and intangible—do you want from your job?

Some people want to feel connected with others; some want to make significant contributions; some want to be acknowledged for their efforts. There are no right or wrong answers to these questions.

It may be possible to get the things you want from your present job. People often think that they need to change jobs to upgrade quality. However, don't ignore the opportunity to find satisfaction by changing some part of your current job or looking for ways to enrich the work.

In our focus on the big rewards we want in our jobs, we sometimes overlook the intangible rewards and satisfaction our jobs provide. In *Mr. Holland's Opus*, Richard Dreyfuss played a passionate musical composer who must take a job teaching music in a high school. He dreamt of one day composing a truly memorable work of music, but obstacle after obstacle forced him to continue teaching. During most of his career, he focused on his failure to fulfill his dream of composing his opus and didn't see the contribution he made daily to the lives of his students. At a surprise party, Mr. Holland realized his impact on the generations of young people he had inspired during his career as a music teacher. He had created a legacy as meaningful and long-lasting as his dream opus.

Redefine Success

Success is a fluid concept. The way you define success for yourself today may be different from the way you define it in the future. Many of my clients discover that what they wanted a few years ago is not what they want today. Think about your definition of success. After you have used your new scripts for a while, I encourage you to return to this definition and see if it still fits. If it has changed, redefine success. There is no right or wrong answer; today's answer may turn into something else. It can—and should—change as you and your circumstances change.

Velma was amazed that a year after her promotion to vice president of sales and marketing, she wasn't excited about a new opportunity to run an overseas marketing division of her multinational company. Five years earlier, when she first came to me to strategize her goals for success, the opportunity would have been her dream job. She came back to me to for coaching on her latest dilemma. She didn't want her dream job now. The year before, she had married a wonderful man. Now she dreamed of becoming pregnant and raising a family. Her current position is perfect for her and is in balance with her personal life and goals. Velma needed reassurance that it was all right to change her goals. You, too, may find that yesterday's goals—like your outdated beliefs—no longer fit who you are today.

The Process of Change

The road to change is never straight, and the journey along that road has many surprises—detours, traffic jams, stop lights, roadside attractions, even occasional fender-benders. As you change your scripts to change your response to situations, you move along in fits and starts. You move two steps forward, one step backward. You feel you have made progress today, then you backslide tomorrow. Sometimes fear and anxiety will drive you back to your old comfort zones—which are only comfortable because they are familiar.

You are going through a period of transition that William Bridges describes so beautifully in his book *Transitions*. The transition is that awkward period when you are moving from your old, familiar scripts—and the roles you have played for many years—to your new scripts and new roles. You are keenly aware of where you have been, or where you are coming from, but you haven't completely arrived where you want to be. You have to go through a period of adjusting and reorienting yourself to a new self-image.

This adjusting and reorienting period takes time, and you need to be patient with yourself as you sputter along. It took a lifetime to get to where you are today. It is unrealistic for you to expect yourself to change overnight. You have built and polished your role for years; doing something completely different can be a shock to your well-rehearsed system.

As your parents did before you, you are doing the best you can. If you had more understanding and awareness, you would do things differently. You create habits and problems to fulfill a need in you. When you can find a positive way to fulfill the need, you can release the problem.

You can't speed up the process of adjusting to change. It has its own natural pace. You may find that some changes are easier for you than others. Going through the phases of internal discovery, recognition, growth, and change will take you out of your comfort zone, and some shame, embarrassment, and awkwardness can be expected in any stage of growth. Whatever the pace of your change, it is best if you can show yourself the patience, loving kindness, and positive encouragement you might show a child who is learning to walk. Recognize that change is a gradual process, and give yourself the time and space to put your new scripts in place.

Use Optimistic Thinking

Change happens when you make it happen. You make the commitment to change, and from commitment springs the empowerment you need to achieve your goals.

You must trust and believe that you can change. It is important during any transition phase to maintain an optimistic outlook. Pessimistic thoughts you concoct about your ability to change will undermine you. Thinking "I'll never get it right" or "I'm too old; I can't change" won't serve you. Backsliding does not mean that all your efforts are in vain; it doesn't mean you can't change; it doesn't mean you are a failure. Negative, pessimistic thoughts are like the villains in a movie who will try to convince you to give up as soon as things feel uncomfortable. You can replace your pessimistic thoughts with optimistic ones. Focus optimistically on your ability to change, and you will change.

When you do backslide, stay in the present. Acknowledge and own the part of yourself that has reverted to the old role. Something is going on that you need to investigate before you can proceed. The fact that you do recognize you have taken a step back is actually an indication that you are making progress.

I think of backsliding as going back to the old neighborhood. You are just visiting; you are not living there anymore. Your new discomfort with the negative events in your life shows that you don't want to live in that old neighborhood anymore; you don't even belong there anymore.

Now it is uncomfortable there, so celebrate that discomfort. It shows you no longer have a high tolerance for negativity. Say to yourself, "Okay, here's that old familiar movie set that brought me so much misery. Is this where I want to stay?"

If you don't, figure out what you need to do to get back on track.

Sometimes events send you rushing back to old, familiar habits and scripts. For example, seeing your parents and relatives, or visiting your childhood home, can reactivate all the scripts you thought you had rewritten. An event of high emotional intensity—a divorce, a layoff, being fired, an illness, a death in the family—can sometimes compel us to return to our old, familiar ways. You are especially vulnerable when you are in that transitional period of releasing the old script and learning the new script.

When you backslide, it is easy to feel discouraged. You may think you are doomed to suffer, or that all the progress you have made has vanished. But the new script is there; it hasn't gone away! This is a momentary lapse. Go back to your success journal and celebrate all the progress you have made so far. Recognize that the old feelings and behaviors are signs that you have more work to do. Dig back into past to see what script you are using and what the point of your pain is. It's like peeling back the layers of an onion: the layers represent all your years of experience, beliefs, and emotions. You have to go through the first layer to get to the second, the second to get the third, the third to get to the fourth.

When you find yourself reverting to old scripts, remember that you always have a choice. You don't have to remain stuck repeating those old lines from old movies you have grown weary of playing. You can intervene—call in the director and find out what's going on. Call in the cinematographer, pull back to a wide-angle view, and look through the objective lens. Call in the writer and brainstorm another way to write this part of the script. Maybe you are still holding on to something because you haven't finished grieving for it yet. Maybe you haven't come up with something to replace it with. Ponder the situation. What are you afraid of losing? What can you replace it with?

Seek the Support of Others

Undergoing change is usually made easier when you have the support of others. We really *do* benefit from others; they are like mirrors reflecting our own transition and success back to us. Think about the people you can turn to during your transition period who can offer guidance and positive reinforcement for the changes you are making. A trusted and admired co-worker, friend, or spouse can offer you a new perspective, remind you of your goals, and share the pride of your accomplishments.

If you are really stuck, other resources can help you. A minister, rabbi, or religious advisor may offer an objective viewpoint and advice. If you feel that the source of your problems may be a poor career choice, a career counselor can help identify something more suitable. A professional counselor can help you sort out emotional issues that overwhelm you or are too painful for you to examine by yourself.

Be kind to yourself and hold the optimistic belief that you can change. Don't beat yourself up for the setbacks; instead, renew your commitment to change and seek support.

Dealing with a Relapse

Tony, the sales rep, relapsed. When he took a new position that offered more money at a different company, he began drinking again. Although he was excited about his new challenges, his anxiety about his ability to succeed filled him with fright, and he began to drown his anxious feelings in alcohol.

Fortunately, Tony knew from our counseling sessions that he had some choices. He could choose to take the pessimistic route—"Here I go again. I'll never be sober. I'll never get what I want!"—and throw away his chances for success; or he could choose to intervene. That is what put him back on the path to success.

His first step was to go back to Alcoholics Anonymous. He knew he would reconnect with people there who would support him during this difficult phase. Then he focused again on disputing his pessimistic thinking. He disputed his belief that life consisted of limited resources. He disputed his tendency to see things in the black-and-white terms of *always* or *never*. He forced himself to look at the situation more realistically.

When the negative thoughts and feelings came up, he thought, "Cut! I don't have to fill myself with blame and guilt. Okay, I've had a relapse, but the most important thing right now is to resume being sober and to focus on my goals. I know I can be a successful sales manager."

As in many great movie dramas, Tony lived on a roller coaster for a while. He had more than one relapse. He went into another spell of drinking, and his new job was threatened. Tony had reached that tough layer of the onion. He had to peel back this layer to go deeper into what was causing him to revert to his old scripts when he knew they sabotaged his success.

In this layer, he discovered that he resented that he couldn't enjoy a few drinks at the local bar as other men did. He recognized this resentment as another familiar childhood feeling. As a boy, he wished his parents were like the other kids' parents. Their parents weren't negative like his father and deeply religious like his mother. His long-cherished wish was to be just like the other kids—and as an adult, he still wanted to be just like the other guys.

But he is not. He must let go of this unrealistic wish, stop feeling sorry for himself, and realize that he can't have the career success he wants unless he stays clean and sober. He needs to learn that when he goes out to celebrate with others, he can't celebrate with alcohol. Each successful evening when he sticks to juice and mineral water, he will gain more strength to keep on the track of sobriety, one day at a time.

Tony also needs to recognize that he is vulnerable to anxiety when success—meeting or beating a sales goal—is on the horizon. These events trigger his old coping strategies. This is when he must be especially vigilant about using his new scripts. Each new challenge spawns a new fear, and the temptation to ease the anxiety with alcohol will follow. Tony will have to keep re hearsing, rewriting, and refining his script. It will become easier with each round, but it will still require his deliberate attention and commitment to succeed.

You Are at Risk For Certain Feelings

Strong negative feelings that come up, such as feelings of being hurt, left out, or disappointed, are scar tissue from an old injury. If you hurt your knee years ago skiing or playing football, you may feel pain for the rest of your life. A slight accident, such as bumping your knee against the coffee table, reactivates the pain. Your knee doesn't hurt as much as it did when you originally injured it, but it still aches; and you know your knee will always be sensitive to certain kinds of movements or stresses.

It's the same with our feelings—with our emotional injuries. When certain old pains get aggravated, old negative feelings from childhood come flooding back. For example, Nora, the information security consultant, is always vulnerable to feeling rejected by others when they ignore her suggestions. This is her sore spot.

While the feelings never go away, you do become more adept at coping with them. You become quicker at figuring out what is going on and calling on the director and camera person to help you analyze, reframe, and refocus the situation. You recognize *you* are in charge now; you have taken the reins of power from the child of the past. You can choose how you wish to respond instead of letting the feelings sabotage your behavior.

Become aware of situations that are likely to stir up old feelings and reactivate your old scripts. This can happen whenever you are entering familiar turf, where all the old cues and feelings reside. For example, starting a new job may bring back anxiety because you feel like the new kid on the block who doesn't know anyone. Losing a boss you really liked may bring up feelings of loss and abandonment, as well as insecurity about how the new boss will view you. Being assigned to a new project might reactivate feelings of incompetence. Old feelings may arise as soon as you leave your comfort zone, but now you have the tools to deal with them.

Start With One Small Change

Remember that making a change doesn't happen in one big *whoosh*! All big events, from construction of a high-rise building to the making of an award-winning movie, start with small actions. Think about any project you have worked on: it is a compilation of many small tasks, each building upon others and all coming together to create a significant impact. At work, if you can do just one thing differently, that one change can have a wide-ranging impact.

For example, say you have a problem expressing your ideas in staff meetings and taking credit where you should be taking credit. A proactive step would be to prepare before you even go into that meeting. Do just one thing during the meeting that you will feel pleased about at the meeting's end. You will feel successful, and you can build on that success. Celebrate each small success. Eventually the small successes will add up to major victories.

Remember Simone, who made self-deprecating remarks about her great ideas. She made just one change by introducing her ideas with "Here's my idea" instead of "This is probably a stupid idea." Her feelings about her ideas and herself began to change quickly. She also began thanking people when they complimented her instead of passing it off with "It was nothing." Little changes and successes built up, and with each small change she took ownership for her creativity and her personal power.

Celebrate Each Success

Celebrate each day. Celebrate each success, no matter how small. Use your daily success journal to review your progress and give yourself credit for each effort to change.

The first big step to making any change is to recognize what you are doing right now. When you can see that you are creating or contributing to your problem, you have taken that huge first step. Some people never take it. Give yourself a reward for stepping in the direction of success. Continue to reward yourself for each step you take to create success at work.

The Lights! Camera! Action! steps I've described in this book will serve you throughout your life. When things are not working the way you would like, here are the steps to keep in mind:

Lights: Recognize what you are doing and how you are hurting or sabotaging yourself. What is your part in the scene? Recognize your irrational beliefs and thoughts.

Camera: Focus and reframe. Look at the scene differently. Release old faulty beliefs, thinking, and feelings. Use the lens of optimism to give you a bright new view. Identify your choices.

Action: Use the new script and new behaviors. Practice to make the new script familiar and comfortable for you. Continue in your crucial role as director.

Remember that life is a continual process. Until we draw our last breath on this planet, we continue to change, to grow, to evolve, and to be that glorious work in progress.

References

Bandler, Richard. *Using Your Brain—for a Change*. Moab, Utah: Real People Press, 1985.

Bridges, William. *JobShift: How to Prosper in a Workplace without Jobs*. Reading, Mass.: Addison-Wesley, 1994.

Cudney, Milton R., and Robert E. Hardy. *Self Defeating Behavior*. San Francisco: Harper, 1991.

Edelstein, Michael R. *Three-Minute Therapy*. Lakewood, Colo.: Glenbridge Publishing, 1997.

Ellis, Albert, and Ralph Harper. *A Guide to Rational Living*. New York: Institute of Rational Living, 1961.

Engel, Lewis, and Tom Ferguson. *Hidden Guilt*. (Previously called *Imaginary Crimes*.) New York: Pocket Books, 1990.

Frankl, Viktor. *Man's Search for Meaning*. Boston: Beacon Press, n.d.

Garfield, Charles. *Second to None*. New York: Avon Books, 1992.

Gillett, Richard. *Change Your Mind, Change Your World*. New York: Simon & Schuster, 1992.

Golman, Daniel. *Emotional Intelligence*. New York: Bantam Books, 1995.

Jeffers, Susan. *Feel the Fear and Do It Anyway*. New York: Fawcett Columbine, 1987.

Kriegel, Robert, and David Brandt. *Sacred Cows Make the Best Burgers*. New York: Warner Books, 1996.

Pritchett, Price. *New Work Habits for a Radically Changing World*. Dallas: Pritchett & Associates, 1994.

Seligman, Martin E. P. *Learned Optimism*. New York: Pocket Books, 1990.

Senge, Peter M. *The Fifth Discipline: The Art and Practice of the Learning Organization*. New York: Doubleday, 1990.

Stoltz, Paul G. *Adversity Quotient*. New York: John Wiley & Sons, 1997.

Woititz, Janet Geringer. *Home Away From Home*. Pompano Beach, Fla.: Health Comm, 1987.

Suggested Resources

You may find these books helpful as you work on creating success in your life.

Beattie, Melody. *Codependent No More*. New York: Harper/Hazelden, 1987.

Bolles, Richard Nelson. *What Color Is Your Parachute?* Berkeley: Ten Speed Press, 1996.

Braham, Barbara J. *Calm Down: How to Manage Stress at Work*. Glenview, Ill.: Scott Foresman, 1990.

Bramson, Robert M. *Coping with Difficult People*. New York: Ballantine Books, 1981.

Bridges, William. *Transitions: Making Sense of Life's Changes*. Reading, Mass.: Addison-Wesley, 1980.

——. *Managing Transitions*. Reading, Mass: Addison-Wesley, 1991.

Canfield, Jack, and Mark Victor Hansen. *The Aladdin Factor*. New York: Berkley Books, 1995.

Chopra, Deepak. *The Seven Spiritual Laws of Success*. San Rafael, Calif.: Amber-Allen Publishing, 1994.

Covey, Stephen R. *The Seven Habits of Highly Effective People*. New York: Simon & Schuster, 1989.

Dempsey, Mary H., and Rene Thista. *Dear Job Stressed*. Palo Alto: Davies Black Publishing, 1996.

Dyer, Wayne W. *Your Erroneous Zones*. New York: Perennial Press, 1976.

Elgin, Suzette Haden. *The Gentle Art of Verbal Self Defense*. Englewood Cliffs, New Jersey: Prentice-Hall, 1980.

Hanson, Peter G. *Stress for Success*. New York: Ballantine Books, 1991.

Isachsen, Olaf, and Linda V. Berens. *Working Together*. Coronado, Calif.: New World Management Press, 1988.

Jaffee, Dennis T., and Cynthia D. Scott. *Take This Job and Love It*. New York: Simon & Schuster, 1988.

Kelley, Robert E. *How to Be a Star at Work*. New York: Times Books, 1998.

Kiersey, David, and Marilyn Bates. *Please Understand Me*. Del Mar, Calif.: Prometheus Nemesis Book Company, 1984.

Kroeger, Otto, with Janet M. Thuesen. *Type Talk at Work*. New York: Dell Publishing, 1992.

Lakein, Alan. *How to Get Control of Your Time and Your Life*. New York: Signet, 1974.

Lerner, Harriet Goldhor. *The Dance of Anger*. New York: Harper & Row, 1985.

Meyer, Isabel Briggs. *Gifts Differing*. Palo Alto: Consulting Psychologists Press, 1980.

Miller, Marlene. *Brain Style—Change Your Life without Changing Who You Are*. New York: Simon & Schuster, 1997.

Noer, David M. *Healing the Wounds*. San Francisco: Jossey-Bass, 1993.

Ray, Samuel N. *Job Hunting after 50*. New York: John Wiley & Sons, 1991.

Ross, Ruth. *The Prospering Woman*. Mill Valley, Calif.: Whatever Publishing, 1982.

Scott, Cynthia D., and Dennis T. Jaffee. *Managing Personal Change*. Los Altos, Calif.: Crisp Publications, 1989.

Seligman, Martin E. P. *What You Can Change and What You Can't*. New York: Ballantine Books, 1993.

Shapiro, Francine, and Margot Silk Forrest. *EMDR: The Breakthrough Therapy*. New York: Basic Books, 1997.

Sher, Barbara, with Barbara Smith. *I Could Do Anything if I Only Knew What It Was*. New York: Dell Publishing, 1994.

Sinetar, Marsha. *Do What You Love, the Money Will Follow*. New York: Paulist Press, 1987.

Wieder, Marcia. *Making Your Dreams Come True*. New York: MasterMedia Limited, 1993.

Index

About the Authors

Rochelle Teising, MFCC, CEAP, is a founding partner of Success At Work, a San Francisco-based consulting group providing high-performance coaching and seminars for organizations. She has worked in the field of employee assistance counseling and has traveled extensively, consulting with executives, managers, and employees on improving the quality of working relationships and communication skills. She has served as a consultant to such diverse organizations as medical centers, an international oil company, sales and marketing companies, technology and research firms, manufacturers, medical and law practices, and nonprofit agencies.

Catherine Joseph is a communications consultant and writer. She has written on topics ranging from managing change, career transition, and job search techniques to corporate culture, the learning organization disciplines, and information technologies. A former management trainer and outplacement counselor, she has spoken on and conducted seminars on supervision, communications, and career management.

Success at Work provides the following services: personal coaching to break through blocking beliefs and barriers to success; seminars to assist in optimistic explanatory styles for increased productivity; conflict resolution and mediation services for enhanced employee relations; team-building for work groups. For more information on these services contact Rochelle Teising at 415-693-0630 • 220 Montgomery Street, Suite 317 • San Francisco CA 94104

Rochelle Teising has a special talent for helping folks discover the "part" they play in their personal success. The direct application of this discovery to the work setting results in increased job satisfaction and increased performance effectiveness.
—*Christie Holt*
   Consultant, High Performance Organizations, Chevron Products Co.

Rochelle Teising has the rare ability to see both the business and human sides of workplace problems. Even rarer, she is able to assist in bringing problems to successful closure.
—*Sara Barnes, MSW*
   Human Resources Manager, InfoWorld Media Group
   Adjunct Professor, University of San Francisco, McLaren School of Business

A truly remarkable book that captures the essence of what it takes to be successful not only in business, but in life.
—*Tom Eager*
   Global Sales Manager, Portables & Storage, 3M Electronics Products Division

On numerous occasions I've observed with awe Rochelle's true talent in influencing individuals and teams at all organizational levels. The results have always been improved working relationships and business performance.
—*Robert J. Valentino*
   President, The Napa Group

Rochelle has the special ability to move people past the "internal obstacles" that might inhibit their success in the workplace.
—*Debbie Kolhede*
  Senior Vice President, Clinical & Administrative Services, Mt. Diablo Medical Center

In handling employee relations issues over the years, I have definitely seen more people who have derailed their careers due to self-destructive behaviors and interpersonal conflict in the workplace than those who have failed due to inadequate technical skills. Rochelle Teising's work will be invaluable to anyone who may be self-sabotaging his or her career by carrying around their own hidden roadblocks to success. It should be required reading for any manager who is serious about pursuing a career path without self-imposed limits.
—*Nancy Cryer Wennerberg*
  Director of Human Resources, The Westin Santa Clara